Pie is Messy

RECIPES FROM
the
PIE HOLE

REBECCA GRASLEY

WITH WILLY BLACKMORE

PHOTOGRAPHS BY
ANTHONY TAHLIER

TEN SPEED PRESS
California | New York

contents

THIS BOOK IS DEDICATED TO

My grandson, Jordan Deemer, who is my smile and my heart, and the reason I do all things.

My mother, Elaine Pursel, who continues to amaze me with her energy and determination.

My son and my daughter, Matthew and Jennifer Heffner, and all my family and extended family who supported my journey with their love.

My love, Ben Baltrusaitis, whose strength and kindness keep me grounded through it all.

And all the guests who frequent the Pie Hole shops and warm my soul with their pleasure in eating pie!

Left to right: Becky's great-great-nephew Ray Kile, Becky, and her great-great-niece Stella Kile.

introduction

A SMALL PIE SHOP

When my two children were young, we baked together. And while we baked, I told them about my dream of opening a pie shop, which the three of us—Jennifer, Matty, and myself—would run. It wouldn't be our own place, I'd tell them as I stood on the gray-and-red-tiled kitchen floor of our white clapboard house in Berwick, a small town in Northeast Pennsylvania, watching the two of them try to cut shortening into flour. No, just a corner of someone else's store. A couch, a coffee pot, a few pies we baked the night before. While they were at school, I'd go to our shop down on Front Street, with its stately old brick buildings. And when the pies were all gone, I would put up a Sold Out sign and return home. Then, after their homework was done that night, we'd gather around the old Formica-topped pedestal table in the kitchen and bake for the next day.

That was the dream: a little pie shop in the corner of a store.

I started baking with my kids when they were toddlers, just as I learned to bake standing on a chair at my grandmother's side. It was the late 1970s, and I didn't have a stand mixer back then, or even a food processor. Instead, my kids and I made piecrust the old-fashioned way: Everything was dumped into an old pink-and-blue-striped ceramic bowl that was big enough for two pairs of tiny hands and my pastry blender. The kids would perch on chairs around the table while we baked, and invariably dusted the whole room (and themselves!) with flour. While the pie was in the oven, I cleaned up the kids, scraping dough off the backs of their hands with a butter knife. I had to spend nearly as long a time as it took to bake the pie cleaning everyone. It was a mess, but I wouldn't have had it any other way.

Making pie wasn't just a pastime or a hobby in Northeast Pennsylvania—it was part of the fabric of life. There were pies after church, pies at family picnics, pies in the big glass case at the counter of the diner, pies upon pies at the holidays, and even pie, rather than cake, at birthday parties. Getting together with a bunch of people? Bring a pie!

A lot of the fruit we used for summer pies was grown nearby, but we never announced that the ingredients were local—it was just the way things were done. Everyone had a garden patch in Nescopeck, the town near Berwick where I grew up, and lots of people sold their produce out by the side of the road, at a little stand with an honor

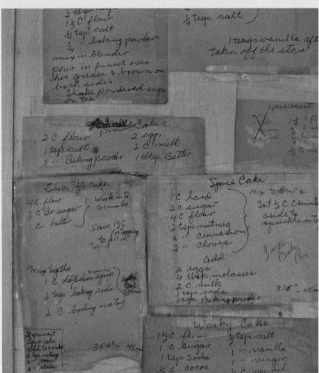

box to stuff cash in. (No one was ever there to ring you up or count out change, but no one ever seemed to take advantage.) We had to drive across the river to Berwick to go to a grocery store, so it was a lot more convenient to grow a bit of our own fruits and vegetables and shop at the roadside farm stands instead—not to mention more delicious. You could get a bunch of rhubarb that was already cleaned and ready to chop up for pie or grab a little basket of peaches.

There was always something that could be baked up in a crust.

When my kids were a little older, we left Pennsylvania and moved to New Jersey. It was still pie country, but pie was usually something you made and enjoyed at home, rather than a dish that you might bring to a potluck or a church event. I was living away from family, and trying to make new family where and when I could. So I would still bring pie to an event, and it would be a huge hit because people weren't expecting it. I was always the one who brought the pie, the Pie Lady.

Over the years I baked thousands of pies, but the small pie shop didn't happen. I've reinvented myself many times, working in a factory, then as a nurse, while doing the never-ending work of being a mom. My kids grew up, and our family spread out across the country.

Jennifer still lives on the East Coast, where she is raising Jordan, my only grandson, and Matty moved to California. While Jennifer is now quite happy to make pie with a store-bought crust and canned filling, Matty has always loved to bake from scratch. Whenever he'd come home to the East Coast for a visit, we'd make pie together, just like we did years ago when he had to stand on a chair to reach the countertop.

In 2010, during a Thanksgiving get-together at a hunting estate in Michigan, Matty and I did what we always do, baked and baked. The whole extended family was staying in cabins scattered around the huge property, and for three days we made pie after pie in the cast-iron kitchen stove in the main lodge: pecan, lemon meringue, chocolate with graham cracker crust, double-crust apple, cherry, blueberry, coconut cream, custard, shoofly, and pumpkin. At Thanksgiving dinner, everyone insisted that I ought to open a pie shop.

My son and I talked about a pie shop whenever we baked together, but always as a joke or a dream for the distant future. That November, however, the idea became more real as we watched everyone enjoy the abundance of pies. We talked about a shop again, and this time, we decided to take the plunge. My son wanted to call the business Pie Hard, which would be followed by Pie Hard with a Vengeance. But we ultimately landed on the Pie Hole, a reference to my habit of telling the kids to shut their pie holes when they were growing up.

Like so many other people, I had lost a lot of my retirement savings when the stock market tanked in 2008, a year after I retired from my job as a nurse. I didn't have enough to live on, but I did have enough to invest in myself. We decided that we'd open in Los Angeles, where Matty lived, which presented a more lively retail market than Berwick. Unlike Berwick folks, a whole lot of people in L.A. would be very happy to buy a homemade pie.

Then came the moment of no return. I flew out to L.A. in March 2011, where I met my son's friend Sean Brennan, who had experience opening restaurants. He became not only a co-owner but also like another son to me. I cashed out my retirement savings and opened a business account. Matty and I were finally going to have that small pie shop we dreamed about.

We opened the shop in Los Angeles's Arts District, which is a far cry from old-school Front Street in Berwick, with its Newberry five-and-dime and Montgomery Ward (both long shuttered). Instead, the Pie Hole counted converted warehouse loft spaces, galleries, and boutiques as its neighbors. With its wooden tables, butcher-paper menu, and hip, tattooed staff, the bakery fit right in. And although it looked a little different from our old vision of a couch, a coffee pot, and a few homemade pies, we're very much that family-run shop at heart.

I still swear by my Grandma Moe's crust, which is the foundation of nearly every Pie Hole pie. The family recipes are our building blocks. At the Pie Hole you can eat the kinds of pies you'd find at reunions and church lunches in Northeast Pennsylvania. The Blue Ribbon Apple Pie (page 44), for example, is my grandmother's recipe, which won the blue ribbon at a New Jersey State Fair in the 1980s. Others, like our Spiced Hot Chocolate Pie (page 131), take a classic cream pie and update it with flavors you probably don't expect to find in a pie. Our Maple Custard Pie (page 194) has become the favorite of my mother, Elaine, who scoffed at the idea before she tried it.

Whether you're eating my family recipes or the inventive, modern pies we serve alongside the classics; whether you're ordering a slice in a Pie Hole in Pasadena or Hollywood or Tokyo or somewhere in the Middle East, you'll be in a comfortable, friendly place where you can enjoy a slice of pie and a cup of coffee. We have never lost touch with this ideal, which is at the heart of the business. Now, with the help of this cookbook, you can enjoy the same experience in your own home.

I want this cookbook to be your go to book for all your pies. My hope is that you use these margins to jot down your own notes when baking. Like tips and tricks you learned to make your efforts a success, a maybe adjustments you make for your family to cater to their taste. Enjoy the journey! Enjoy your pies 😊

In a way, running the Pie Hole is like those days when I made pies with my kids and cleaned off their dough-covered hands. The one thing I keep telling the team is this: pie is messy. If a slice of blueberry pie is oozing filling out of the sides rather than sitting on the plate like a perfect, pert triangle, that is perfectly okay. Life is messy, and that's what makes it good. Everyone at the Pie Hole knows that, and it's become our motto or mantra. Our director of operations, Bianca Molina, the Pie Hole's longest-serving and much loved and respected employee, even had it tattooed on her in the official brand font: Pie Is Messy.

It's something that we've all come back to time and again over the years. Like when Thanksgiving is a few days out and it seems like there are a million more pies that need to be baked, and *then* a whole pie gets pulled out of the cooler to be sliced, only to end up splattered all over the floor. Or when a member of the team is obsessing over a slice of pie for a guest, I'll bring it up again: It doesn't have to be just so, because pie is messy. "Pie is messy" is a reminder that not everything has to be perfect in order to be good, or even great. And it applies beyond the particular business and stress that comes with running a bakery. In fact, pie making has saved me repeatedly throughout my life, before the Pie Hole came into existence. It has made tough times more bearable, good times even better, and family closer. Whether you've never baked a pie or have baked hundreds, my hope is that this book will help you make your own wonderful memories and maybe even give you a boost when you need one.

THE PIE PANTRY

There isn't much of a difference between your average pantry and a pie pantry. You don't need to stock any fancy flours or hard-to-find fruits. Mostly pies are made from ingredients that you probably have in your kitchen right now. Are there eggs and milk in the fridge, and flour and cornstarch in the cabinet? You've got the beginning of a custard pie or a cream pie. Is there a bowl of fruit sitting on the counter that will soon be overripe? Make a fruit pie out of the fruit. If you become a Pie Lady like me, ingredients will come your way all on their own. People routinely hand off bunches of berries or apples that are going to go bad, knowing they'll be tucked into a crust. But even if no one in your neighborhood gives you pie-making gifts, you'll need to buy only a few ingredients, say pecans for a pecan pie, or blueberries for a blueberry pie.

Growing up, what we had on hand was more ruled by the seasons than things are today, and between that and the holiday calendar, it was usually pretty obvious what pies we'd make at what time of year. Everything is available all year round now, even in the Northeast, but out-of-season ingredients are more expensive and tend not to taste very good either. So while you *could* make a peach pie in February with fresh peaches, if an overwhelming urge struck, it's not going to be your best choice. You'd be better off baking a Chocolate Cream Pie (page 114) instead—I promise you that a slice of Peach-Basil Pie (page 53) will taste far superior on a sticky day in late July.

But crust ingredients, thickeners, and other pie staples do not change with the season. And once you've stocked up on a few basics, it will be easier to bake a pie when the mood strikes—whether it's a holiday classic, a seasonally appropriate favorite, or something more out of left field.

I keep salted butter in my fridge, and I never buy unsalted for the sake of a recipe, because I find them almost interchangeable. If you're a salted butter person, you're in luck here, because it's the only type of butter I call for, aside from vegan. And if you buy only unsalted, you'll probably be just fine using that instead.

EQUIPMENT

A lot of my baking equipment was handed down from my grandparents. But that's not to say that everything needs to be a family heirloom, much as I may love my grandmother's old glass lemon juicer. I may be sentimental, but sentimentality isn't what makes good pies!

More than anything, it's about having the right tools and equipment, not the oldest, or the fanciest, or the most expensive. And while it's nice to have that stand mixer, it's not something you absolutely need.

PIE PANS

I am definitely partial to pie pans—the heavy-duty metal ones that can last you a lifetime, not the flimsy disposable kind made from aluminum foil. For years I've collected vintage ones from back when they were made of tin—including my most prized pan from the Frisbie Pie Company, which made tins that flew through the air so well when thrown that they evolved into the toy. These days most pie pans are made from aluminized or enameled steel, and the metal is a good heat conductor, which allows the fat in your pie dough to melt (and create steam) quickly, resulting in a flaky piecrust. I prefer metal pie pans to Pyrex because I find the crust takes longer to bake in glass, and you get a less flaky crust as a result. Metal pie pans are also better for getting a fully baked—and evenly browned—bottom crust.

If you're shopping for pie pans, you probably want to head for the restaurant supply store rather than a fancy cookware shop—ceramic and stoneware pans can be very pretty, but you really don't need to spend that much. Look for something sturdy that doesn't have any kind of nonstick coating—I don't want that stuff touching my crust, and pies have enough fat in them that they very rarely stick to aluminized or enameled steel pans. Granite Ware makes very affordable enameled pie pans that are basically indestructible, and USA Pans is another good brand to look for.

Pies are canonically round—but that doesn't mean that they have to be. You can make square pies, rectangular pies, or free-form galettes that are as individual as snowflakes. If you have a pan or dish that's oven safe and you can lay a piecrust into it, you can use it to make a pie. But for the sake of the recipes in this book, the instructions assume that you'll be baking your pie in a 9-inch pie pan (unless otherwise noted).

FOR THE CRUST

All-purpose flour

Graham crackers

Salted butter

Vegetable shortening

FOR THE FILLING

Coconut flakes

Eggs

Fruit

Peanut butter

Pecans

Sugar

**Unsweetened chocolate
(I like Baker's)**

**Unsweetened cocoa
(I like Hershey's)**

Vanilla extract

Walnuts

TO THICKEN
THE FILLING

Cornstarch

Gelatin

Quick-cooking tapioca

ROLLING PIN

I prefer old-fashioned wood rolling pins, the kind with handles that really roll, not the tapered, solid-wood French kind. Mine was my grandmother's, and I inherited it after she died in 1994. She had given me other ones before, but this was her favorite, and now it's the one I always use.

BOWLS

You don't have to go out and buy anything special. I have one big old ceramic bowl—the same one that my kids crammed their little hands into when we baked together—and a few stainless-steel bowls in different sizes. That's all you'll need.

PASTRY BLENDER

There are plenty of ways to cut fat into flour, and every baker seems to have their personal preference, from fingertips to a food processor. By my measure, the best and easiest tool to use is a handheld pastry blender. The thick wires on the business end make quick work of cutting cold shortening into flour, and they do it more evenly than if you were to use your hands. There's also less mess to clean up compared to using your fingers, or a food processor. A stand mixer is my go-to when I have to make many pies—but if you're making a crust for just one pie, a pastry blender is ideal.

FLUTED PASTRY CUTTER

If you're looking for one of these in a kitchenware store or searching online, you'll want to call it a "fluted pastry cutter." But in my kitchen, it's a wavy noodle cutter, because when you use this tool to cut dough, it makes what look like wavy noodles. It's a handy tool for cutting pie dough into strips that will be woven together for a lattice-top crust.

EVERYTHING ELSE

You'll need measuring cups and measuring spoons, and a scale might come in handy here and there. It's nice to have a few wooden spoons for mixing, too.

CHAPTER 1
the crust

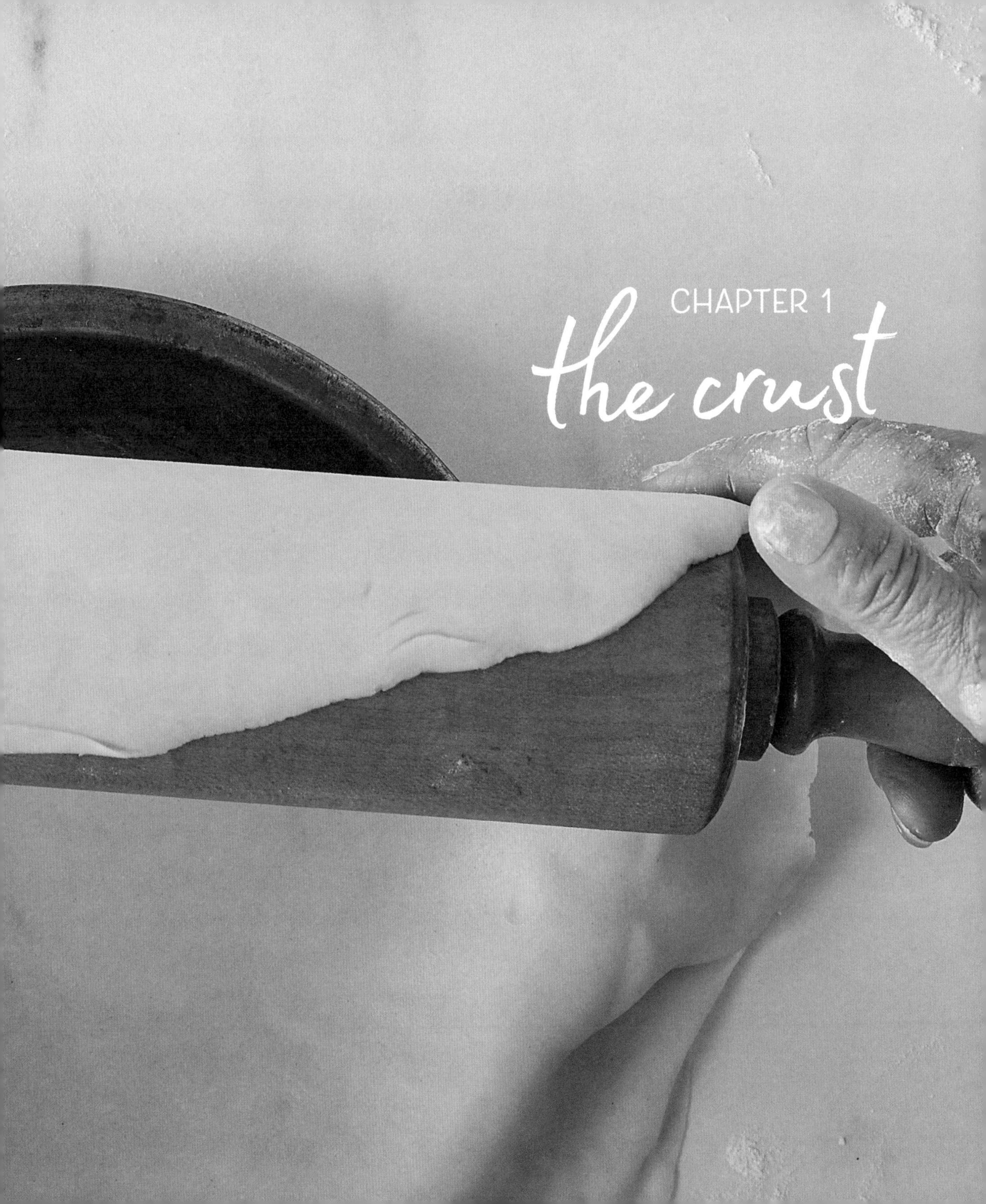

meet moe

At the Pie Hole, we use Moe's Piecrust (page 19), the recipe my grandmother Moe swore by. Well, it isn't exactly the same way Moe made it—she used a full cup of lard instead of butter or shortening. That was pretty standard for home bakers of her generation, who grew up during the Depression. Butter was seen as a luxury and was treated as such in the kitchen. I remember her telling me stories about how families were given tubs of white fat with a yellow coloring packet. They were supposed to blend the dye into the grease to help fool themselves into thinking that it was actual butter. She never got onboard with that, and preferred to use plain old lard instead, which remained both cheap and readily available throughout the 1930s and '40s. Even decades after butter was once again an affordable kitchen staple, she still used lard for both pies and cakes. I can see why. To me, lard is perfection in a crust—no other fat makes pastry so flaky. It's what I still use for savory pies. But ironically, today lard isn't as readily available, and the fact that it's a meat product is a turnoff for some. So shortening it is.

Moe (her name was Grace, but everyone called her Moe) had six kids, so there were a lot of us grandchildren. I was just one of the horde who went over to her house on Sundays after church or for holidays. She was a strict, small woman, no more than five feet tall—and was famous for her roast chicken (she and my grandfather Steve, who we called Pop, raised their own birds) and for her baking, pies in particular. She was always in her spotless kitchen, where the gray-and-green-speckled linoleum floor had worn away in front of the stove and sink, thanks to the many hours she spent standing at both.

Moe and her daughters (*left to right*): Ruby Masanotti, Grace (Moe) Kacyon, Elaine Pursel (Becky's mom), and Nancy Hart.

I'd always look for a reason to be in there with Moe so I could watch and sometimes help as she baked. But I had to be careful to stay out of her way, because if I didn't, I'd be met with a withering frown. She didn't have to say anything; that look was enough. But even if she wasn't warm and fuzzy, I was fascinated by her.

Tucked into the corner, next to the counter, was a low wooden kitchen table (Pop had shortened the legs with his saw), which tiny Moe stood and worked at. She always wore a full apron with a gingham or floral print, which I thought of as a cape. The way that she worked with dough I could have sworn she was a superhero. She was so quick with her hands, kneading and rolling and lining a pie pan with dough in a matter of seconds. Moe would regularly whip out four piecrusts like that—sometimes as many as eight— and then fill them with pureed pumpkin or mincemeat for Thanksgiving or Christmas, or chocolate pudding for a Sunday lunch with the family. She always made tons and tons of food and baked goods because she had a large family to feed. And later in life she sometimes still cooked in those quantities, out of confusion (and maybe habit, too), even though it was just her and her Pop living at home.

You don't need a pie-baking grandmother or your own cherished family recipe to make a good crust—not if you have Moe's Piecrust recipe, that is. Nothing stresses out novice pie makers more than making the crust, but it's a more forgiving process than people think. After all, there's a reason for the expression "as easy as pie." Sure, you need the shortening to be cold, and you need to work quickly when you're cutting it into the flour. But none of that means it needs to be intimidating. Really and truly, you can make a piecrust, and a good one at that. The trick is to keep the fat cold and to work quickly.

Even after all these years of baking, occasionally, I still end up with piecrusts that are too sticky or too dry. If that happens to you, and you figure out how to make it work, then you've learned something. I'm still learning. As long as you can flour it and roll it out, and it doesn't stick to the counter, you can use it.

If you are making the crust in a stand mixer, use the dough hook instead of the pastry paddle. That might seem counterintuitive, but trust me: a flaky crust starts by combining flour and fat into a mealy mixture, and the dough hook, which does a better job of mimicking the cutting action of a pastry blender, will get you there. Using the paddle will leave you with a flour-and-butter mixture that is too smooth.

MOE'S PIECRUST

Use this recipe for one double-crust pie, like the Blue Ribbon Apple Pie (page 44), or two single-crust pies. You'll need at least half a batch—one ball of chilled dough, ready to be rolled out—for most recipes in this book. Because the way the crust is treated before it's filled varies from one pie to the next (parbaked, fully baked, or not at all), the particulars are addressed in each recipe. But these are the pages you'll want to refer to for instructions on how to mix the dough, chill it, and roll it out.

1. In a large bowl, mix the flour, shortening, and salt with a pastry blender until crumbly, and the bits of flour and fat are the size of peas.

2. Sprinkle the ice water over the mixture, starting with ½ cup, and, using your hands, quickly mix the dough until it comes together in clumps and you can shape it into a ball. If the mixture is still too crumbly, add more cold water, 1 tablespoon at a time. Watch the texture as you mix. When the dough becomes smooth and velvety, like a baby's behind, it's time to stop working it. If you do happen to overmix the dough, and it resembles an elastic blob, don't stress. You'll still enjoy the pie in the end, even if the crust isn't perfect. And next time you'll get this step just right.

3. Alternatively, use your stand mixer fitted with the dough hook attachment. On low speed, combine the flour and salt. Mix in the shortening, increasing the speed up to medium as the fat begins to combine into the flour. Stop when the mixture turns grainy—if it becomes a smooth paste, you've gone too far—2 to 3 minutes. Switch to the paddle attachment and add ½ cup of ice water. Mix on medium, and add more ice water, 1 tablespoon at a time, until the dough turns smooth and soft.

4. Divide the dough into two balls, wrap in plastic wrap, and store in the refrigerator for at least 30 minutes, or until you are ready to roll out the crust.

continued ⟶

MAKES ENOUGH FOR ONE 9-INCH DOUBLE-CRUST PIE OR TWO 9-INCH SINGLE-CRUST PIES

3 cups all-purpose flour

1 cup cold vegetable shortening

1 teaspoon kosher salt

½ cup ice-cold water, plus more as needed

There's a bit of a learning curve to adding the ice water to the fat and flour. The amount of liquid you need may vary, depending on the humidity. The only way to get a really good feel for it is to make a lot of pies. I always start with ½ cup of ice-cold water for a full recipe of Moe's Piecrust and usually need a few extra splashes. As long as the water is very cold, the crust will still be forgiving, even if you are too heavy-handed with the liquid. Although you can make piecrust with water straight from the tap, the extra step of icing will give you a flakier crust.

ROLLING OUT THE DOUGH

Mixing the dough is one thing; making it into a piecrust is another. It's a little more involved, but this, too, is more forgiving than people will have you believe.

Lightly flour the work surface, and flatten one ball of the chilled dough. I use the side of my hand to hit the dough with a few karate chops, rotating the dough to make a sort of hashtag sign on it and smoosh it into a flat circle. Next, flip it over and use a rolling pin to roll out what I like to call a starfish pattern on the round of dough: start in the middle of the dough and roll out to one "arm," then go back to the middle of the dough and roll out to the head of the starfish, and so on. Repeat for all five points on the starfish. Unlike simply rolling back and forth, this pattern will actually give you a circle of dough instead of a weird oblong that's hard to fit into a pie pan.

Flip the dough over and repeat, starting again from the middle and rolling out to each limb of the starfish. There's no exact point at which you are done rolling out the crust. The thickness is a matter of personal preference, and with each pie you bake, you'll get a better sense of what works best for you. But if you're brand new to pie making, roll out your crust into a circle that's about 11 inches in diameter and is just shy of ¼ inch thick. After a lifetime of making pie, I can do all of this so quickly that I'm like a pie ninja—karate chop, flip, and roll, roll, roll. It takes some practice, but you'll get there, too.

I use my rolling pin to transfer the crust into the pie pan: start with the rolling pin a few inches from the top of the dough, and fold the small arc on the far side of it back onto the pin. Slowly pull the pin back toward yourself, rolling the dough onto it as you go, and continue until you have the whole crust draped onto the rolling pin. You'll want to have your pie pan close at hand so you don't have to keep the crust on there for long! Starting at the edge of the pie pan closest to you and moving away from yourself, start unrolling the crust. Once you have all of the crust off the rolling pin, gently adjust the dough until you have an even overhang all around the pan.

continued —→

FLUTING THE EDGE

To flute a single pie shell, trim the edge of the dough so that you have ¾ to 1 inch overhanging the edge of the pie pan—and be sure to set aside those trimmings to make Piecrust Cookies (page 30) with later. (This is a matter of personal preference; I like a thick crust, so I leave about 1 inch.) Gently pinch a few inches of the overhanging dough in both hands and use your thumbs to roll it underneath itself, continuing up to the top edge of the pan, creating the beginning of a lip on the edge of the pie shell. Move along, rolling up the overhanging dough a few inches at a time, until you have a smooth lip around the crust.

Now you're ready to flute the crust. If you're right-handed, press your left thumb and index finger gently on the lip of the crust, and use your right index finger to push the rolled-up dough down into the space in between your two fingers, making an indentation on the lip. (If you're left-handed, just do the reverse.) Move one finger width away from the first indentation and repeat. You'll start to see the wavy pattern of a fluted edge. Continue in this way until the fluting runs all the way around the rim of the crust.

For a double-crust pie, trim the edge of the bottom crust just as you would for a single crust, but don't flute it yet. Add the pie filling. Roll out the top crust and cut vents in it *before* you place it on top of the pie filling. That way, you're cutting on a flat surface instead of running a knife over the bumpy, wet filling. You don't need to do anything special in cutting the vents: just use a butter knife to poke a few holes (they don't need to be any longer than ½ inch) in the top crust to allow the steam to escape as the pie bakes. (Otherwise, it may explode in the oven.) After cutting the vents, place the top crust over the pie, and trim so that the top crust is ½ inch larger than the bottom crust. Use your fingers to fold the overhanging top crust under the slightly smaller bottom crust, and pinch it to form a seal. After sealing the two crusts together all the way around, flute the edge as you would for a single-crust pie.

If I'm making several kinds of double-crust pies and I'm trying to remember what's what, I use the dull side of a butter knife to label them. I trace an *A* into the unbaked top crust if it's an apple pie, and a *B* for blueberry. But I don't cut all the way through the dough. I just leave an impression on it.

continued —>

DECORATING THE CRUST

I rarely decorate my pies beyond fluting the edge of the crusts. There are a few exceptions: around Valentine's Day I'll put a few hearts along the edge of a pie, made from rolled-out scraps of dough. Or I use my turkey-shaped cookie cutter to make a dough bird and place it in the middle of a Thanksgiving pumpkin pie before I bake it, but that's the vast minority of pies that I bake in a year. I always thought the fluted crust is pretty enough on its own.

If you really want to go all out, you can customize the top crust by spelling out a person's name in pie dough letters—a perfect touch for a birthday pie. Normally, I don't use an egg wash on my pies, but an egg beaten with 1 or 2 tablespoons of water is the perfect glue for sticking the letters to the crust, and I'll use whatever I have left to coat the rest of the piecrust, too. That will give your letters and the crust a nice burnished look, but egg wash doesn't add anything beyond that caramel color.

LATTICE TOP

You actually weave strips of dough together to make a lattice-top crust, which takes extra time, so it's not something that we regularly do at the Pie Hole. But at home, the extra effort really pays off, especially for a cherry or blueberry pie, because the filling looks particularly pretty showing through the lattice.

Before you begin the lattice top, roll out the bottom crust, transfer it to the pie pan, and trim the dough, but do not flute the edge. Fill the pie shell. To make the lattice top, start by rolling out your top crust as you normally would. Then use a fluted pastry cutter ("wavy noodle cutter"; see page 10) to cut the round of dough into strips about 1 inch wide. Pick out 12 strips that are long enough to be placed across the filling, with a 1-inch overhang on each side of the crust. Place half the strips across the filling vertically, ½ inch to 1 inch apart, with the shorter strips on the left and right sides and the longest strips running down the middle.

Fold up every other strip from the halfway point of the pie, so that there are only four strips covering the bottom half of the pie. Place a strip horizontally across the middle filling so that it lays over the vertical strips you didn't fold. Unfold the other vertical strips over the horizontal one. You now have one strip of dough woven into your lattice! Repeat the process, but this time, fold up the vertical strips that you didn't fold up the first time. Continue weaving horizontal strips across the vertical

continued ⟶

ones in this manner, making sure that you alternate the vertical strips you flip up—that's the key to creating the weave. One you finish the first half of the pie, repeat the same process on the other half to complete the lattice.

After you've laid the last horizontal strip of dough, tuck the ends of the lattice top underneath the overhanging edge of the bottom crust, and pinch to seal. Roll under and flute the edge of the crust, just as you would with a normal double-crust pie.

PARBAKING A SINGLE CRUST

Most recipes for one-crust pies with a very wet filling call for a parbaked crust. Partially baking the crust before it is filled ensures that the filling won't bleed through the crust before the heat of the oven sets it. To parbake the crust, preheat the oven to 375°F. Roll out the crust and carefully lay it in the pan. Use the tines of a fork to poke holes in the bottom and sides, which will keep the crust from bubbling. Bake for 15 to 20 minutes, or until the crust is set but not browned, and cool on a rack. I don't use pie weights or beans—if it shrinks, it shrinks.

For recipes that call for a fully baked crust, bake for 35 to 40 minutes, or until golden brown.

OTHER CRUSTS

You could bake practically every recipe in this book using Moe's Piecrust (page 19), and you'd have yourself a delicious pie. But there are a few very important exceptions. Take the Key Lime Pie (page 175), which you simply cannot make without a graham cracker crust. The crumbly texture and the almost toasted flavor of the cracker meal is part of what makes key lime pie great. So while you *could* fill Moe's crust with a batch of lime cream, it wouldn't make a ton of sense to do so. There are the old-school pies that break with the classic crust—including key lime and nearly all the cream pies—and new-school recipes like Vegan Coconut Cream Pie (page 159), with a crust made exclusively of sweetened coconut flakes and coconut oil. We make piecrust from vanilla wafers and Oreos at the Pie Hole, too. But we use graham crackers far more frequently.

I recently bought a stainless-steel pie-weight chain, and after a lifetime of not weighting down my crusts during parbaking, I am now mildly converted. Unlike other pie-weight hacks, like using dry beans bundled up in plastic wrap or resting on a layer of tinfoil, it doesn't involve extra layers or barriers—the chain just lies right on top of the crust. The cleanup is quick, too—just soap and water. You really don't need to buy a pie-weight chain to make a pie, especially if you're just starting out. But it's nice to have around.

GRAHAM CRACKER PIECRUST

MAKES ENOUGH FOR ONE 9-INCH PIE

This crust is dead simple: you grind up graham crackers, mix the crumbs with sugar and butter, press the mixture into a pie pan, and bake. That's it! No fussing over cutting in fat or rolling out dough. The only moment when a graham cracker piecrust can go wrong is right after it comes out of the oven. During baking, the crust will slide down the sides of the pan, leaving you with something rather sad and deflated looking. The trick to having your finished pie *not* look like that is to immediately reshape the crust once it is done baking. You don't want to touch a just-baked crust, which will be red hot, but the perfect tool for this is already in your kitchen: a metal spoon. The rounded back is perfectly shaped for pushing the crust back up the sides of the pan.

9 to 10 graham crackers, broken into pieces (I like Honey Maid)

¼ cup sugar

6 tablespoons salted butter, at room temperature

1. Preheat the oven to 350°F.

2. In a food processor, pulverize the graham crackers into a coarse meal. The texture should be something like brown sugar—you don't want any big, discernible chunks of cracker, and you don't want it to be so fine that it resembles flour. Alternatively, you can put the crackers in a ziplock bag, push as much of the air out as possible, and run a rolling pin back and forth over the bag until they're crushed. Set aside 1½ cups of the cracker crumbs, and discard the rest or save it for another use.

3. In a large bowl, combine the graham cracker crumbs and sugar. Use your hands to combine the butter with the cracker crumbs by squeezing and smooshing the softened butter into the sugar and cracker crumbs until the mixture comes together like a dough. You're done mixing when it sticks together if you squeeze a pinch between your fingers.

4. Dump the dough into a 9-inch pie pan and use your fingertips to press it evenly over the bottom and up the sides of the pan. You want to make sure the thickness of the crust is uniform, particularly where the bottom meets the side.

5. Bake for 5 minutes, or until the bottom looks shiny with melted butter. Immediately reshape the crust using the back of a metal spoon (the crust will be too hot to use your fingers). The sides will slip down during baking, and the sooner you press them back up, the better the shape of the final crust will be. Cool on a rack for at least 30 minutes before filling.

PIECRUST COOKIES

There are always a few odd bits of pie dough left over after rolling out crusts, and while they're not enough to make another pie, they can still make beautifully flaky treats. My kids always loved it when I made these piecrust cookies for them after we were done making our pies.

**Piecrust scraps, from
1 piecrust recipe**

**Salted butter, at room
temperature**

Ground cinnamon

Sugar

1. Preheat the oven to 400°F. Line a cookie sheet with parchment paper.

2. Gather the piecrust scraps, ball them up together, and roll out your leftover dough into a rectangle, or as near as you can get it, with a long side facing you. Cover the surface lightly with a bit of room-temperature butter—you can use your fingertips to spread it around—and sprinkle all over with cinnamon and sugar. The amount of cinnamon sugar will vary, depending on the amount of dough you have. You want the dough to be well covered, like cinnamon toast.

3. Starting at the long side of the rectangle nearest you, roll up the dough tightly into a log. Slice into pinwheels 1 to 1½ inches thick, and place on the prepared cookie sheet.

4. Bake for 10 to 12 minutes, or until golden brown. A sheet of these cookies can be tucked in alongside a pie or a parbaking crust, if you have the room. Cool on a rack for at least 30 minutes—I often eat these while they're still warm—or to room temperature, about 2 hours.

CHAPTER 2

fruit pies

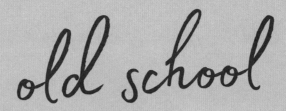

old school

When my kids were in grade school, we moved from Pennsylvania to an old dairy farm in Hunterdon County, New Jersey. There were a few hundred acres of pastures, all of which were leased out, but we had the farmhouse and the bit of land surrounding it, complete with a stocked fishing pond, a creek, and a big old barn that the kids liked to play in.

Growing on the property were a number of berry bushes. I wasn't sure what type of berries they were, but I knew they were edible. So the kids would pick them, and we'd put them into pies. Sometimes they were impossibly seedy, other times they were perfect. I used a version of my blueberry pie recipe for our mystery berry pies. I would take the berries, toss them with some sugar, lemon juice, and a bit of cornstarch or tapioca, dump them into a piecrust, and bake. It was always an experiment, but that was part of the fun.

Like those New Jersey berry pies, most fruit pie fillings have three main ingredients: fruit, sugar, and some kind of thickener, like flour or tapioca. The sugar helps draw the liquid out of the fruit, and the combination of the thickener and the heat of the oven turns that liquid all gooey as the pie bakes. Whether berry, cherry, apple, or another kind of fruit, the result is similar: you end up with tender pieces of sweetened fruit, held together loosely by a jammy sauce. Sandwiched between layers of flaky piecrust, a fruit pie can be one of the simplest, most delicious desserts imaginable.

This approach works no matter what kind of fruit you have on hand: whether a few pints of mystery berries instead of blueberries, a couple bundles of rhubarb and no strawberries, or nectarines instead of peaches, you can make a fruit pie.

CHERRY PIE

Moe's Piecrust (page 19)

1 quart sour cherries, pitted

1¼ cups sugar

2½ tablespoons all-purpose flour

¼ teaspoon kosher salt

We don't make cherry pie very often in the Pie Hole kitchen because it takes so much time to pit the fruit. But while it's a lot of work, fresh cherry pie is absolutely worth it. You absolutely do need sour cherries—Montmorency is the most commonly grown variety, but whatever you can get will work—for this recipe, not sweet cherries. There's a reason, after all, that sour cherries are also called pie cherries! Their acidity is tempered a bit by both the sugar that's in the filling and the time in the oven, leaving you with the classic cherry pie flavor.

I use only a touch of flour in the filling. So don't expect it to be like the slices of cherry pie you get at the grocery store or restaurant that are cut into perfect straight-edged triangles—I don't know what they put in those. Cutting the pie might be a bit messy, but once people are eating, no one seems to care that the filling is oozing out all over the place.

Pitting cherries is the kind of slow work that's drudgery in a commercial kitchen but feels like peak summer when done on the porch during a long, lazy afternoon. There are plenty of cherry-pitting tools you can buy, but all you really need is a nut pick or a chopstick. Poke the tapered end through the side of the cherry and use your other hand to squeeze and roll the flesh until the pit pops out. Alternatively, you can use one hand to make the same squeezing/rolling motion and pull on the stem with the other. Once you get the hang of it, you can pop out the pit and pull off the stem all at the same time. Be sure to buy extra cherries, so you can eat a handful or two as you work.

1. Preheat the oven to 400°F.

2. Roll out two rounds of dough for the bottom and top crusts, and lay the bottom crust in a 9-inch pie pan.

3. In a large bowl, combine the cherries, sugar, flour, and salt. Pour the filling into the bottom crust and trim the edge. Make slits in the top crust and lay it over the filling. Alternatively, you can make a lattice top (see page 24). Pinch the edges of the two crusts together to seal, and flute according to the instructions on page 23.

4. Place the pie on a cookie sheet (to catch the drips) and bake for 10 minutes. Lower the heat to 350°F and bake for 25 minutes longer, or until the cherry juice is bubbling up out of the slits in the crust and the top is golden.

5. Serve the pie warm, or cool on the counter until room temperature, about 2 hours.

BLUEBERRY PIE

I've always put a bit of nutmeg in my blueberry pie, because that's the way Moe made hers. And for the longest time, I thought that was the way all blueberry pies are made. That's certainly not the case, and sometimes when people taste it, it catches them off-guard—it's always a bit of a surprise. The difference starts with the smell of the pie baking, which has a much richer aroma than you'd expect from a fruit pie. And the flavor is so much more layered with nutmeg, which brings out the earthy flavor that really good blueberries have. As far as I'm concerned, nutmeg is almost as essential for a blueberry pie as the berries themselves.

1 quart fresh blueberries

¾ to 1 cup sugar

3 tablespoons all-purpose flour

½ teaspoon grated lemon zest

⅛ teaspoon freshly grated nutmeg

Pinch of kosher salt

Moe's Piecrust (page 19)

1 teaspoon freshly squeezed lemon juice

1 tablespoon salted butter, cut into tiny cubes

1. Preheat the oven to 400°F.

2. In a large bowl, combine the blueberries, sugar, flour, lemon zest, nutmeg, and salt. Stir together gently. You'll see how quickly the sugar starts to draw the juice out of the berries, especially if you accidentally crush a few with the spoon. That delicious juice, thickened by the flour, will make the filling jammy in the finished pie.

3. Roll out one round of dough for the bottom crust. Lay the bottom crust in a 9-inch pie pan, and trim the edge. Dump the berry mixture into the bottom crust, sprinkle the lemon juice over the top, and dot with the butter. Roll out the second round of dough for the top crust, make slits in it, and lay it over the filling. Pinch the edges of the two crusts together to seal, and flute according to the instructions on page 23.

4. Place the pie on a cookie sheet (to catch the drips) and bake for 35 to 40 minutes, or until the top is golden brown and the filling is bubbling up through the slits.

5. Serve the pie warm, or cool on the counter until room temperature, about 2 hours.

BLUEBERRY CRUMB PIE

½ recipe Moe's Piecrust
(page 19)

Filling

1 quart fresh blueberries

¾ to 1 cup sugar

3 tablespoons all-purpose
flour

½ teaspoon grated
lemon zest

1 teaspoon freshly
squeezed lemon juice

⅛ teaspoon freshly
grated nutmeg

Pinch of kosher salt

Crumb Topping

⅓ cup sugar

¾ cup all-purpose flour

6 tablespoons salted butter

The only time I make a blueberry crumb pie is when I don't have quite enough
fruit for a regular blueberry pie. If I can't mound the berries in the middle,
I mound a crumb topping over the blueberries instead. When it's all browned
and crispy, the topping adds a wonderful bit of texture to each bite of soft,
tart fruit.

1. Preheat the oven to 400°F.

2. Roll out the crust, and lay it in a 9-inch pie pan. Trim and flute the edge according
to the instructions on page 23. Set aside.

3. To make the filling: In a large bowl, combine the berries, sugar, flour, lemon zest
and juice, nutmeg, and salt. Stir together and pour the mixture into the crust.

4. To make the crumb topping: In a medium bowl, mix together the sugar and flour.
With a pastry blender or your fingers, work in the butter until the mixture is crumbly.
Mound the crumb topping over the berry filling.

5. Place the pie on a cookie sheet (to catch the drips) and bake for 10 minutes. Lower
the heat to 350°F and bake for 25 minutes longer, or until the filling bubbles up
through the topping and the crumb turns golden brown.

6. Serve the pie warm, or cool on the counter until room temperature, about 2 hours.

RHUBARB PIE

One of my earliest baking memories is of making rhubarb pie with Mom Pursel, my very loving grandmother, who was about as different from prickly Moe as she could be. I was about five years old, and we were chopping up rhubarb at the counter when I cut my finger rather badly. My grandmother was pretty worked up and was fussing over me. I guess that should be a bad memory, but it isn't. I don't remember the pain, just the love, and her trying to make it all better. So oddly enough, cutting my finger while making rhubarb pie is part of what makes me like rhubarb pie.

1. Preheat the oven to 400°F.

2. In a large bowl, stir together the sugar, tapioca, and salt. Add the rhubarb and mix to coat the fruit. Let the rhubarb mixture stand for about 20 minutes, allowing the sugar to draw out the liquid from the rhubarb.

3. While the rhubarb sits, prepare the crust: Roll out two rounds of dough for the bottom and top crusts. Lay the bottom crust in a 9-inch pie pan, and trim the edge.

4. Dump in the rhubarb mixture, and dot the top with pieces of butter. Make slits in the top crust and place it over the filling. Pinch the edges of the two crusts together to seal, and flute the edge according to the instructions on page 23. Alternatively, you can make a lattice top (see page 24), if you want the pie to be extra pretty.

5. Place the pie on a cookie sheet (to catch the drips) and bake for 35 to 40 minutes, or until the crust is nicely browned and the rhubarb is very tender.

6. Serve the pie warm, or cool on the counter until room temperature, about 2 hours.

1½ cups sugar

3 tablespoons quick-cooking tapioca

¼ teaspoon kosher salt

1½ pounds rhubarb, cut into ½-inch pieces (about 3 cups)

Moe's Piecrust (page 19)

1 tablespoon salted butter

I love the tartness of a straight-up rhubarb filling, but if you aren't looking for a dessert that will make your mouth pucker, you can always temper the filling with fresh strawberries. Follow the rhubarb pie recipe but reduce the amount of rhubarb to 1 pound and add 1 cup of sliced strawberries to the filling.

BLUE RIBBON APPLE PIE

MAKES ONE
9-INCH PIE

1 cup sugar, plus more
for sprinkling

2 heaping tablespoons
all-purpose flour

1 teaspoon ground
cinnamon

Pinch of kosher salt

8 tart apples, such
as McIntosh, peeled,
cored, and thinly
sliced (about 6 cups)

Moe's Piecrust (page 19)

2 tablespoons salted
butter, cut into tiny cubes

My Favorite Whipped
Cream (optional; opposite)
for serving

When we lived in New Jersey in the 1980s, there wasn't always a ton of money. So I found ways to stretch and pinch while still managing to have fun with the kids. Which is why I would enter a pie in the baking competition at the state fair every summer: contestants and their families got into the fair for free. But after the rides and the games, we didn't head for the food carts for funnel cakes and corn dogs—as far as my kids were concerned, that part of the festivities didn't even exist. Instead, it was back out to the parking lot, where we'd set up a little hibachi grill by the car to cook up hot dogs or burgers. I'd bring along some potato salad or pasta salad and a few bags of chips. And for dessert we'd eat the pie that got us all into the fair in the first place, minus the one small slice removed for judging purposes.

But that final part of my thrifty scheme didn't pan out the year I won a blue ribbon for my apple pie. When I returned to the exhibition hall to collect the pie, I was told there was nothing left. The judges had liked it so much that they ate every last bit.

1. Preheat the oven to 400°F.

2. In a large bowl, combine the sugar, flour, cinnamon, and salt. Add the apples and mix until the fruit is thoroughly coated with the sugar mixture.

3. Roll out two rounds of dough for the bottom and top crusts. Lay the bottom crust in a 9-inch pie pan, and trim the edge. Fill the crust with the apple mixture and dot the top with the butter.

4. Cut slits in the top crust and lay it over the filling. Pinch the edges of the two crusts together to seal, and flute the edge according to the instructions on page 23. Sprinkle the top with a little sugar. Place the pie on a cookie sheet (to catch the drips) and bake for 50 minutes.

5. Serve the pie warm, or cool on the counter until room temperature, about 2 hours. Either way, serve with whipped cream, if you'd like.

MY FAVORITE WHIPPED CREAM

MAKES
2 CUPS

Good whipped cream is all about timing. Chill the bowl first in the refrigerator, and whip the cream as close to serving time as possible. Do both, and you'll end up with the most perfectly fluffy whipped cream. (Or, you could leave it unsweetened, as some people in Northeast Pennsylvania prefer.)

1 cup heavy cream

3 tablespoons confectioners' sugar

½ teaspoon vanilla extract

1. Chill a large metal bowl in the refrigerator for 15 minutes. Pour in the cream and use an electric mixer on medium speed to beat until the cream starts to thicken. Increase the speed to medium-high and continue beating until the cream holds soft peaks.

2. Add the confectioners' sugar and vanilla and continue to beat until the cream is stiff, but not grainy. Refrigerate until needed, but no more than 2 or 3 hours. If whipped cream sits for too long, it will separate slightly. If it does, whip for 10 or 15 seconds before serving.

APPLE-CHEDDAR PIE

In my family we often serve apple pie with a slice of Cheddar, especially during the holidays. Mincemeat always gets a slice of cheese on top of the tart, too. It's an old English tradition, cheese on pie, which somehow worked its way down the generations to our corner of Pennsylvania. I don't know if it started with one of my English ancestors, but I do know that I love it—a nice strong, sharp cheese contrasts so well with a sweet fruit filling like mincemeat or apple. Instead of just putting a slice on top of the finished pie, I work grated cheese into the crust, too. That way, you get the more toasty, melted flavor of the cheese.

Cheddar Piecrust

3 cups all-purpose flour

1 cup cold vegetable shortening

1 teaspoon kosher salt

2 cups shredded sharp Cheddar cheese

½ cup ice-cold water, plus more as needed

Filling

8 tart apples, such as Gala or Cortland, peeled, cored, and thinly sliced (about 6 cups)

¾ cup sugar

2 tablespoons quick-cooking tapioca

¾ teaspoon ground cinnamon

Pinch of kosher salt

2 tablespoons salted butter, cut into tiny cubes

8 ounces sharp Cheddar cheese, sliced, for serving

1. To make the Cheddar piecrust: In a large bowl, mix the flour, shortening, and salt with a pastry blender until crumbly, and the bits of flour and fat are the size of peas. Add the shredded cheese and stir. Sprinkle the ice water over the mixture and use a wooden spoon to stir until it all comes together. If the mixture is still too crumbly, add more cold water, 1 tablespoon at a time, and stir until it clumps together into a ball. Divide into two balls, wrap in plastic wrap, and refrigerate while you make the filling.

2. Preheat the oven to 400°F.

3. To make the filling: In a large bowl, toss together the apples, sugar, tapioca, cinnamon, and salt. Set aside.

4. Roll out the two balls of dough for the bottom and top crusts. Lay the bottom crust in a 9-inch pie pan, and trim the edge. Spoon the apple mixture into the pie shell and dot the top with the butter. Make slits in the top crust and lay it over the filling. Pinch the edges of the two crusts together to seal, and flute according to the instructions on page 23.

5. Place the pie on a cookie sheet (to catch the drips) and bake for 20 minutes. Lower the oven temperature to 350°F and bake for 35 to 45 minutes longer, or until the crust is golden brown, the apples are tender, and the bubbles coming up from the filling look thick.

6. Cool on the counter until room temperature, about 2 hours. Serve with a slice of Cheddar on the side.

APPLE CRUMB PIE

Instead of a top crust, you can cover the apples with crumb topping and get the best of both worlds: apple pie and apple crumble at the same time. As much as I love a double-crust apple pie, you can't really appreciate it until you cut into it and see the filling. But since the filling bubbles up through the topping here, the pie really announces itself in a very attractive and appetizing way.

1. Preheat the oven to 400°F.

2. To make the filling: In a large bowl, combine the sugar, flour, cinnamon, and salt. Add the apples and mix until the fruit is thoroughly coated with the sugar mixture.

3. To make the crumb topping: In a medium bowl, stir together the sugar and flour. With a pastry blender or your fingers, work in the butter until the mixture is crumbly.

4. Roll out the crust, and lay it in a 9-inch pie pan. Trim and flute the edge according to the instructions on page 23. Dump in the apple mixture and mound the crumble topping over the top.

5. Place the pie on a cookie sheet (to catch the drips) and bake for 10 minutes. Lower the heat to 350°F and bake for 25 minutes longer, or until the filling bubbles up through the crumb.

6. Serve the pie warm, or cool on the counter until room temperature, about 2 hours.

Filling

1 cup sugar

2 heaping tablespoons all-purpose flour

1 teaspoon ground cinnamon

Kosher salt

8 tart apples, such as Granny Smith or McIntosh, peeled, cored, and thinly sliced (about 6 cups)

Crumb Topping

⅓ cup sugar

¾ cup all-purpose flour

6 tablespoons salted butter

½ recipe Moe's Piecrust (page 19)

PEAR, CRANBERRY, AND GINGER PIE

3 pounds ripe but firm
Bartlett or Bosc pears,
peeled, cored, and
sliced ¼ inch thick
(7 to 8 cups)

½ cup granulated sugar

¾ cup all-purpose flour

¼ cup packed dark
brown sugar

2 tablespoons chopped
crystallized ginger

¾ teaspoon ground ginger

⅛ teaspoon kosher salt

5 tablespoons salted
butter, melted

2 cups fresh or thawed
frozen cranberries, coarsely
chopped

1 teaspoon grated fresh
ginger

½ recipe Moe's Piecrust
(page 19)

This is a nice, warming pie with classic fall flavors that are especially welcome
on Thanksgiving. The pears should be ripe but firm, which means the flesh at
the base of the stem should give slightly when gently pressed. Once I discovered
the trick of cooking the pears in the microwave, this pie became a holiday hit—
meaning I made it more often!

1. Preheat the oven to 400°F.

2. In a large microwave-safe bowl, toss the pears with 2 tablespoons of the granulated
sugar. Cover and microwave on medium for 3 to 5 minutes, until the pears turn
translucent and release their juices, stirring once halfway through the cooking time.
Uncover and set aside to cool completely, about 30 minutes.

3. In a medium bowl, combine 2 tablespoons of the remaining granulated sugar, the
flour, brown sugar, crystallized ginger, ground ginger, and salt. Add the butter and
stir until the mixture is moistened throughout. Cool the topping completely, about
10 minutes.

4. Put the cranberries in a medium bowl. Add the fresh ginger and the remaining
¼ cup granulated sugar. Drain the cooled pears, return to the bowl, and add the
cranberry mixture, stirring to combine. Set aside.

5. Roll out the crust, and lay it in a 9-inch pie pan. Trim and flute the edge according
to the instructions on page 23. Put the fruit mixture in the pie shell, and sprinkle the
topping over the pear mixture, using your fingers to break apart any large clumps.

6. Place the pie on a cookie sheet (to catch the drips) and bake for 45 to 55 minutes,
or until the filling bubbles up through the topping, rotating the pie plate halfway
through baking.

7. Cool completely on the counter, about 2 hours, and serve.

APRICOT-NECTARINE PIE

Filling

1 vanilla bean

1 lemon

¼ cup granulated sugar

Pinch of freshly grated nutmeg

¼ teaspoon ground cinnamon

¼ cup all-purpose flour

Pinch of kosher salt

1 pound nectarines (4 or 5 nectarines), peeled, pitted, and sliced ¼ inch thick

1 pound apricots (5 or 6 apricots)

Crumb Topping

¾ cup all-purpose flour

¼ cup cornmeal

½ cup packed dark brown sugar

Pinch of kosher salt

6 tablespoons salted butter, at room temperature

½ recipe Moe's Piecrust (page 19)

My Favorite Whipped Cream (page 45) or vanilla ice cream for serving

This pie first entered our family repertoire when my mom was a young housewife trying to impress my dad, my brothers, and me. She read magazines like *Family Circle* and *Better Homes & Gardens,* and would cut out the recipes for dishes she wanted to try out. A pie like this was aspirational: we didn't normally have apricots and nectarines around, so the shopping alone made it a special pie.

1. Preheat the oven to 375°F.

2. To make the filling: Cut the vanilla bean in half, and scrape out the seeds. (Save the pod for another use.) Finely grate the lemon zest, and set the lemon aside. Put the granulated sugar in a large bowl, add the vanilla bean seeds and lemon zest, and use your fingers to rub the zest and seeds into the sugar. Stir in the nutmeg, cinnamon, flour, and salt. Add the nectarines to the bowl. Gently tear the apricots in half with your hands, remove the pits, and place the halves in the bowl, too. Halve the zested lemon and squeeze the juice over the top of the fruit. Toss everything together gently to combine.

3. To make the crumb topping: In another bowl, whisk together the flour, cornmeal, brown sugar, and salt until they are well combined. Add the butter and use your fingers to work it into the dry ingredients until large crumbs form.

4. Roll out the crust, and lay it in a 9-inch pie pan. Trim and flute the edge according to the instructions on page 23. Pour the filling into the pie shell, making sure to include all of the juices left in the bowl. Mound the crumb topping over the fruit.

5. Place the pie on a cookie sheet (to catch the drips) and bake for 45 to 55 minutes, or until the crust and crumbs are golden and the filling bubbles.

6. Cool slightly and serve with whipped cream or vanilla ice cream.

PEACH-BASIL PIE

MAKES ONE 9-INCH PIE

When peach season rolls around in Pennsylvania, I usually have basil as tall as a hedge growing in the garden, begging to be used. I tie up a lot to dry for winter, but the picking and trimming and bundling gets tiresome. So I usually tear up a bit and toss it into a peach pie filling, just to mix things up. It's one of those little touches that adds a lot of character to the pie. But you can skip the basil for a classic peach pie. Either way, a lattice top (see page 24) would look nice here instead of a solid top crust.

1. Preheat the oven to 400°F.

2. Blanch the peaches: Fill a large pot halfway with water and bring it to a boil. While the water heats up, set up an ice bath: Fill a large bowl with water and plenty of ice cubes. With the sharp point of a knife, cut an X in the bottom of each peach. Put the peaches in the boiling water for about 1 minute, or until the skins begin to peel back from the cut. Remove the fruit with a slotted spoon and immediately transfer to the ice bath. Once the peaches are cool enough to handle, slip off the skins. Pit the peaches and slice ½ inch thick.

3. Transfer the peaches to a large bowl, and add the sugar, flour, lemon juice, and basil. Stir to combine. Set aside.

4. Roll out two rounds of dough for the bottom and top crusts. Lay the bottom crust in a 9-inch pie pan, and trim the edge. Dump the peach mixture into the bottom crust and dot with the butter. Make slits in the top crust and lay it over the filling. Pinch the edges of the two crusts together to seal, and flute according to the instructions on page 23.

5. Place the pie on a cookie sheet (to catch the drips) and bake for 35 minutes. Lower the oven temperature to 375°F and bake for 30 minutes longer, or until the top crust is nicely browned and the filling is bubbling up through the slits.

6. Cool on the counter until room temperature, about 2 hours, and serve.

3½ pounds ripe but firm peaches (about 8 large peaches)

1 cup sugar

½ cup all-purpose flour

1 tablespoon freshly squeezed lemon juice

2 tablespoons fresh basil, torn into pieces

Moe's Piecrust (page 19)

2 tablespoons salted butter, cut into tiny cubes

PEACH-PRALINE PIE

The addition of pecan praline to this iteration of peach pie is a special touch. The brown sugar and caramel flavors make for a more autumnal and holiday-friendly pie than the Peach-Basil Pie (page 53) or a straight-up peach pie, which is pure summer.

Filling

3 pounds ripe peaches, peeled, pitted, and sliced ½ inch thick (about 4 cups)

½ cup granulated sugar

2 tablespoons quick-cooking tapioca

1 teaspoon freshly squeezed lemon juice

Praline

½ cup all-purpose flour

¼ cup packed dark brown sugar

½ cup chopped pecans

¼ cup salted butter

½ recipe Moe's Piecrust (page 19)

1. Preheat the oven to 400°F.

2. To make the filling: In a large bowl, combine the peaches, granulated sugar, tapioca, and lemon juice. Let stand for 15 minutes.

3. Meanwhile, make the praline: In a small bowl, combine the flour, brown sugar, and pecans, and use your fingers to work in the butter until the mixture is crumbly.

4. Roll out the crust, and lay it in a 9-inch pie pan. Trim and flute the edge according to the instructions on page 23.

5. Sprinkle one-third of the praline mixture over the bottom of the pie shell. Cover with the peach filling, and sprinkle the remaining praline mixture on top, allowing the peach layer to show.

6. Place the pie on a cookie sheet (to catch the drips) and bake for 10 minutes. Lower the heat to 350°F and bake for 20 minutes longer, or until the peaches are tender and the topping is golden.

7. Serve the pie warm, or cool on the counter until room temperature, about 2 hours.

FRESH STRAWBERRY PIE

MAKES ONE
9-INCH PIE

This fresh strawberry pie is what put the Pie Hole on the map in Los Angeles. It has all of that bright, summery flavor of the best California berries, but without any of the sogginess that's often a hallmark of desserts made with juicy strawberries. Not only is this pie delicious, it's easy to make, too. You just hull the berries so they have a flat top, and arrange some of them, pointy-side up, on the crust. Then pour a thickened mixture of mashed strawberries and sugar over the top. The whole strawberries provide a bit of a moisture barrier for the crust, in addition to looking very pretty sticking up out of the mashed berries.

½ recipe Moe's Piecrust (page 19)

1 quart plus 1 pint fresh strawberries

1⅓ cups water

1 cup sugar

3 tablespoons cornstarch

My Favorite Whipped Cream (page 45) for serving

1. Preheat the oven to 375°F.

2. Roll out the crust, and lay it in a 9-inch pie pan. Use the tines of a fork to poke holes in the bottom and sides, which will keep the crust from bubbling. Trim and flute the edge according to the instructions on page 23. Bake for 35 to 40 minutes, or until golden brown. Set aside to cool completely.

3. Hull all the strawberries. One by one, place the strawberries, pointy-side up, in the bottom of the crust, until the bottom is completely covered. In a large bowl, use a potato masher to crush the remaining berries into a puree.

4. In a medium saucepan, combine the crushed strawberries, 1 cup of the water, and the sugar, and bring the mixture to a boil over medium heat, stirring frequently. Meanwhile, in a small bowl, mix together the cornstarch and the remaining ⅓ cup water. Add to the strawberry mixture, and cook for 2 minutes more, or until the strawberry mixture is thick and bubbly. Remove from the heat and set aside to cool completely.

5. Pour the cooled berry mixture over the tops of the whole berries in the pie shell. Refrigerate until completely chilled and the filling is set, about 6 hours. Serve with the whipped cream.

LEMON-PEAR PIE

Moe's Piecrust (page 19)

Filling

1 egg

1 cup sugar

1 teaspoon grated lemon zest

¼ cup freshly squeezed lemon juice

1 tablespoon salted butter

6 to 8 pears, peeled, cored, and cut into small dice (about 6 cups)

I usually make this pie around Thanksgiving, when pears are in season in Pennsylvania. But unlike nearly all of the fruit pies in this book, this is one that can reliably be made with canned fruit if fresh pears aren't available. The combination of the pears and the lemon filling is a little unusual, but it's always a hit once people give it a taste.

1. Preheat the oven to 400°F.

2. Roll out two rounds of dough for the bottom and top crusts. Lay the bottom crust in a 9-inch pie pan, and trim the edge.

3. To make the filling: In a medium saucepan, whisk together the egg, sugar, and lemon zest and juice. Add the butter and cook slowly over low heat, stirring constantly, until the butter has melted and the mixture thickens and bubbles, 3 to 5 minutes. Cook for 2 minutes more and remove from the heat. Set aside.

4. In the bottom crust, arrange the pears in an even layer. Pour the thickened lemon filling over the fruit. Make slits in the top crust and lay it over the filling. Pinch the edges of the two crusts together to seal, and flute according to the instructions on page 23.

5. Place the pie on a cookie sheet (to catch the drips) and bake for 35 minutes, or until the top crust is golden brown.

6. Serve warm out of the oven or chilled (cool on a rack for 2 hours, and then refrigerate for at least 2 hours longer). Both ways are great!

PEAR CRUMB PIE

MAKES ONE 9-INCH PIE

This is the one pie I prefer making with a crumb topping instead of a top crust. It's a texture thing. Bartlett and Bosc pears, which I like to use, have a soft texture. Unlike baking apples, which hold their shape quite well, these pears fall apart. Rather than have a pie full of mush, I prefer the contrast of the sweet, slightly crunchy crumble with the softness of the pear filling.

1. Preheat the oven to 375°F.

2. To make the filling: Put the pears in a large bowl and sprinkle with the lemon juice. Sprinkle the granulated sugar, cinnamon, mace, and flour over the pears, and stir until the fruit is completely coated with the sugar-and-spice mixture and the flour. If the fruit is particularly juicy, the flour might stick only here and there, and if that's the case, add 1 more tablespoon of flour.

3. Roll out the crust, and lay it in a 9-inch pie pan. Trim and flute the edge according to the instructions on page 23. Spoon the pear mixture into the crust.

4. To make the crumb topping: In a small bowl, stir together the flour and brown sugar, and use your fingers to work in the butter. Sprinkle over the filling.

5. Place the pie on a cookie sheet (to catch the drips) and bake for 40 to 45 minutes, or until the topping is lightly browned.

6. Serve the pie warm, or cool on the counter until room temperature, about 2 hours.

Filling

2½ pounds ripe pears, (8 to 10 pears) such as Bartlett or Bosc, peeled, cored, and sliced

1 tablespoon freshly squeezed lemon juice

⅔ cup granulated sugar

1 teaspoon ground cinnamon

¼ teaspoon ground mace

1 tablespoon all-purpose flour, plus more as needed

½ recipe Moe's Piecrust (page 19)

Crumb Topping

1 cup all-purpose flour

⅓ cup packed dark brown sugar

⅓ cup salted butter

DOT'S LEMON SPONGE PIE

1 cup sugar

1 cup whole milk

2 tablespoons all-purpose flour

1½ tablespoons salted butter, melted

1 tablespoon grated lemon zest

Juice of 1 lemon

1 egg, separated

½ recipe Moe's Piecrust (page 19)

Lemon sponge pie is a favorite in rural Northeast Pennsylvania, the only region where you can find it on the menu at local restaurants. Any mom and pop restaurant around Berwick will have it; it's just a staple. This version is an adaptation of the one given to me by my good friend Trudy, who inherited it from her mother, Dot. It was one of those old recipes in which the ingredient list is a little sketchy. For example, it called for "yolk of eggs," but didn't say how many. I've played with it and one egg is just enough.

The filling is simple to make, but it's very unusual. It separates into two lemony layers as it bakes: a creamy layer on the bottom, and the lightest, laciest sponge on the top.

1. Preheat the oven to 400°F.

2. In a large bowl, whisk together the sugar, milk, flour, butter, lemon zest and juice, and the egg yolk until thoroughly combined. In a small bowl, use a handheld electric mixer to beat the egg white until soft peaks form. Gently fold the whipped egg white into the lemon mixture.

3. Roll out the crust, and lay it in a 9-inch pie pan. Trim and flute the edge according to the instructions on page 23. Spoon the filling into the piecrust.

4. Bake for 10 to 15 minutes. Lower the oven temperature to 350°F and bake for 30 minutes longer, or until the top is golden and the middle doesn't jiggle. This pie browns quickly, so be attentive.

5. Cool on a rack for 2 hours, and then refrigerate until completely chilled, at least 4 hours more. Serve cold out of the fridge or bring to room temperature first.

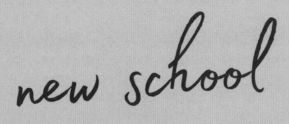
new school

Traditionally, the pie holidays wrap up in December with the final rush of Christmas baking. But after the pumpkin pies and pecan pies have been reduced to crumbs, another exciting and more glamorous season kicks off in Los Angeles—awards season, culminating with the Academy Awards in February. While there's plenty of ceremony around the awards, from the red carpet to the golden statues themselves, the Oscars is not exactly a pie affair, or at least it wasn't until 2018. That's when we decided to come up with a recipe befitting Hollywood's biggest night.

Sarah Chaffin was the chef at the Pie Hole at the time, and she was an incredibly creative force in the kitchen. It was a more formal era for the Pie Hole, when our board meetings doubled as tastings of new recipes, and the pies Sarah presented were picture-perfect. The Oscar pie was no exception. We wanted something incredibly shimmery, like a red-carpet dress or a golden statue. That came courtesy of a bit of gold leaf. While Sarah was developing the recipe, she decided the pie should be raspberry red, and she even worked some sparkling wine into the pie. What she finally presented to the board was the Gold-Dusted Raspberry and Champagne–Cream Cheese Pie (page 81), an Oscar-worthy pie decadent enough to suit the occasion.

Inspired by the incredible breadth and quality of berries, stone fruit, citrus, and more that come from California's farms and orchards, many a new-school fruit pie recipe has been developed at the Pie Hole. The ones in this chapter are riffs on my family recipes, updated with a new flavor combination, or an unusual variety of fruit. Sometimes just a little tweak turns a familiar pie into something fresh and contemporary. Take the Cardamom-Cherry Pie (page 85). It's a classic cherry pie with a dash of cardamom stirred into the filling, which gives it a whole different flavor profile. It's unusual, but it just tastes so good—I prefer it now to my basic cherry pie.

LEMON CREAM CHEESE PIE

I love how the layers look in each slice of this pie: a thin line of vanilla wafer crust, a thick band of cream cheese filling, and a bright yellow cap of rich lemon curd splashed across the top, with a touch of whipped cream on top of that.

Vanilla Wafer Crust

36 vanilla wafers (I like Nilla Wafers)

6 tablespoons salted butter, melted

Lemon Curd

3 egg yolks

¾ cup granulated sugar

1 tablespoon grated lemon zest

¾ cup freshly squeezed lemon juice (2 to 3 lemons)

½ cup salted butter, cut up into cubes

Cream Cheese Filling

One 12-ounce tub cream cheese (not whipped), at room temperature

1¼ cups confectioners' sugar

1 teaspoon vanilla extract

2 cups heavy cream

1. To make the vanilla wafer crust: In a food processor, pulverize the vanilla wafers, pulsing until the cookies are broken down evenly into small crumbs. Transfer to a large bowl, add the butter, and stir until the mixture comes together like a dough. Press into an even layer in the bottom of a 9-inch pie pan. Refrigerate for at least 3 hours.

2. To make the lemon curd: In a large heatproof bowl, whisk together the egg yolks. Set aside. In a medium saucepan, combine the granulated sugar, lemon zest and juice, and cubed butter. Warm over medium-low heat, stirring constantly with a whisk, until the mixture comes to a simmer. Remove from the heat, then temper the egg yolks by slowly ladling the hot liquid into the bowl, whisking constantly, until combined.

3. Return the mixture to the saucepan and continue to cook low and slow, stirring constantly, until the mixture thickens and bubbles start to come to the surface, about 15 minutes. Don't rush it; it takes time to properly thicken the curd. Once the curd is thick and starting to boil, remove the pan from the heat, and push the curd through a fine-mesh sieve into a clean container. Cool to room temperature and refrigerate the lemon curd until ready to use. It will continue to thicken as it cools.

4. To make the cream cheese filling: In a large bowl, combine the cream cheese, ¾ cup of the confectioners' sugar, and the vanilla, and beat with a handheld electric mixer until light and fluffy. In another large bowl, whip the cream with the mixer (be sure to clean the beaters first). As the cream thickens, gradually add the remaining ½ cup confectioners' sugar and whip until the cream forms stiff peaks. Fold half of the whipped cream into the cream cheese filling, and reserve the other half in the refrigerator for serving.

5. Spread the cream cheese filling into the vanilla wafer crust. Spoon the cooled lemon curd on top and spread out evenly with a spatula. Cover lightly with plastic wrap and refrigerate for at least 4 hours before serving.

6. Serve cold, topping each slice with a dollop of the reserved whipped cream.

STRAWBERRY-BLACK SESAME PANNA COTTA PIE

Gray is not a color you expect to see in a pie, but this panna cotta, flavored with nutty black sesame paste, is a good reminder of how beautiful the unexpected hue can be. With its black crust, charcoal-gray filling, and bright-red strawberries covering the top, this pie is really something to look at.

At the Pie Hole, the strawberries are thinly sliced and mounded in the center of the pie. But at home, I like to halve the strawberries and arrange them all over the surface of the filling. There's no need to be precious about the pattern—any way you get them on there will work.

1. Preheat the oven to 300°F.

2. To make the chocolate crust: In a food processor, pulverize the sandwich cookies, cream filling and all. You should have about 1½ cups. Add the butter, and pulse a few times to combine. You'll know the "dough" is done when it starts to clump together in the food processor.

3. Transfer the cookie mixture to a 9-inch pie pan, and use your fingertips to press it evenly over the bottom and up the sides of the pan. You want to make sure the thickness of the crust is uniform, particularly where the bottom meets the sides. Bake for 10 minutes, and then immediately reshape the crust with the back of a metal spoon if the crust has slid down the side of the pan. Set aside.

4. To make the panna cotta: Place a large metal bowl in the freezer to chill. Pour the cold water into a small heatproof bowl, stir in the gelatin, and let sit for 5 minutes. Meanwhile, bring a few cups of water to a boil. Stir the gelatin again, and set the bowl of gelatin water inside a larger heatproof one. Add enough boiling water to come halfway up the sides of the smaller bowl. Stir the gelatin until it dissolves completely, and set aside.

Chocolate Crust

20 cream-filled chocolate sandwich cookies (I like Oreos)

6 tablespoons salted butter, melted

Panna Cotta

¼ cup cold water

1 tablespoon gelatin (1 envelope)

⅔ cup unsweetened canned coconut milk

⅔ cup plus ¾ cup heavy cream

¼ cup sugar

1½ tablespoons pure black sesame paste (I like Nouka)

½ cup fresh strawberries, hulled and halved lengthwise

continued ⟶

5. In a medium saucepan, whisk together the coconut milk, ²⁄₃ cup of the cream, the sugar, and the black sesame paste. Warm over medium heat, stirring occasionally, until bubbles begin to form around the edge of the pan and the liquid begins to steam, about 4 minutes. Remove from the heat and whisk in the gelatin.

6. Take the metal bowl out of the freezer and pour in the black sesame mixture. Refrigerate until cool but not cold—you don't want the gelatin to set yet—about 15 minutes. Whisk in the remaining ¾ cup cream. The mixture should be thick enough to coat the back of a spoon.

7. Pour the panna cotta filling into the chocolate crust and arrange the halved strawberries on the surface. Refrigerate until completely chilled and the filling is set, at least 4 hours.

8. Serve cold.

CANDIED LEMON CHESS PIE

This is based on my recipe for chess pie—the Southern cousin of custard pie—and was greatly improved by the chefs at the Pie Hole. The lemon flavor accents the tart, creamy chess filling, and the candied lemon slices make a beautiful garnish. It's my favorite chess pie recipe.

1. Preheat the oven to 325°F.

2. In a large bowl, combine the sugar, cornmeal, and flour. With a handheld electric mixer running on low, add the eggs, one at a time. Increase the speed to medium and beat until the mixture is pale yellow and slightly foamy, about 5 minutes.

3. Add the butter, lemon juice, and milk. Continue beating until well combined. Stir in the lemon zest.

4. Roll out the crust, and lay it in a 9-inch pie pan. Trim and flute the edge according to the instructions on page 23. Pour the lemon mixture into the crust.

5. Bake for 45 minutes, or until the top is light golden brown and the crust begins to brown. Refrigerate until completely chilled and the filling is set, at least 4 hours.

6. Garnish with the candied lemon slices before serving. You can arrange them however you like. For a circular design, which is what I prefer, start in the middle and lay the slices in concentric and slightly overlapping circles, stopping about ½ inch from the edge of the crust.

7. Serve cold.

2⅔ cups sugar

1 tablespoon plus 1 teaspoon white cornmeal

1 tablespoon plus 1 teaspoon all-purpose flour

6 eggs

6 tablespoons salted butter, melted

⅓ cup freshly squeezed lemon juice

⅓ cup whole milk

2 teaspoons finely grated lemon zest

½ recipe Moe's Piecrust (page 19)

Candied Lemon Slices for garnish (recipe follows)

continued ⟶

MAKES 18 TO
20 LEMON
SLICES

CANDIED LEMON SLICES

1 cup sugar

1 cup water

2 tablespoons freshly
squeezed lemon juice

2 large lemons, cut
crosswise into rounds
⅛ inch thick

1. In a large saucepan, combine the sugar, water, and lemon juice. Bring to a boil, lower the heat to medium-low, and add the lemon slices in a single layer. Simmer the slices for 15 minutes, uncovered, gently flipping once or twice during the cooking process.

2. Remove the lemon slices with a slotted spoon, allowing the syrup to drain into the pan, and transfer the lemon slices to a cooling rack or wax paper to cool. Transfer to a sealed container and store in the fridge for up to 2 weeks.

LEMON–POPPY SEED RICOTTA CHEESECAKE

MAKES ONE 9-INCH PIE

For years I've made ricotta cheesecake from a recipe given to me by an Italian American friend. It's a simple, delicious thing. A few big scoops of ricotta mixed with eggs and sugar make a light filling, which sits on a thin wafer of graham cracker crust. In the hands of former Pie Hole chef Sarah Chaffin, that recipe turned into this lovely variation. The filling is as bright and lemony as ever, and the addition of the poppy seeds gives the pie a little bit of texture and a nice, nutty flavor. It's a little less Italian now, sure, but I still think of my friend whenever I make this version. And I think he'd like the way this one tastes, too.

1. Prepare and bake the graham cracker crust. Set aside. Keep the oven at 350°F.

2. In a large bowl, combine the ricotta, sugar, flour, and vanilla. Use an electric mixer on medium speed to beat until smooth. Add the eggs, cream, lemon zest and juice, and poppy seeds. Beat on low speed just until combined. Pour the filling into the graham cracker crust.

3. Bake for 1 hour, or until the center is almost set but still jiggles a little in the middle and the top looks like it has a suntan. Cool on a rack for 2 hours, and then refrigerate for 4 hours.

4. Serve cold.

Graham Cracker Piecrust (page 29)

2 pounds whole-milk ricotta cheese, at room temperature

1 cup sugar

2 tablespoons all-purpose flour

2½ teaspoons vanilla extract

5 eggs

½ cup heavy cream

1 tablespoon grated lemon zest

¼ cup freshly squeezed lemon juice

⅓ cup poppy seeds

DRUNKEN PLUM FRANGIPANE TART

Drunken Plums

10 plums, halved and pitted (any variety will do)

2 tablespoons salted butter, cut into tiny cubes

¼ cup sugar

2 ounces plum brandy

1 to 2 tablespoons water

2 tablespoons plum jam (or substitute apricot jam)

Frangipane

¾ cup salted butter, at room temperature

¾ cup sugar

3 eggs

¾ cup ground almonds

½ recipe Moe's Piecrust (page 19)

½ cup sliced almonds, toasted

Vanilla ice cream or My Favorite Whipped Cream (page 45) for serving

This is just a beautiful dessert. The glazed, crinkly skins of the roasted plums look so round and soft peeking out of the rustic folds of the free-form tart crust. Looking at it makes you want to pluck a piece of the fruit right out of the middle. But then you'd miss out on the almond layer beneath, which plays so nicely against the sweet-tart flavor of the plums. You really need a full slice, if not two!

This pie always sells out when it's available at one of the shops, but we don't put it on the menu very often—it's a little too labor-intensive for a commercial kitchen. But if you have a basket full of ripe plums at home, it's the perfect recipe.

1. Preheat the oven to 350°F.

2. To make the drunken plums: Lay the plums, cut-side up, on a baking sheet. They should fit snugly, in a single layer. Place a little cube of butter on top of each plum, and sprinkle the plums with the sugar.

3. Dilute the plum brandy with the water and pour over the plums. Roast the fruit for 20 minutes, basting occasionally, until softened and slightly reduced in size, but not collapsing. Remove from the oven, and pour the pan juices into a small saucepan. Set aside the plums to cool.

4. Add the jam to the pan juices in the saucepan. Bring to a boil over medium-high heat, and cook until reduced by half, 5 to 7 minutes. You should have about ½ cup of plum glaze left in the saucepan. Set aside.

continued ⟶

5. To make the frangipane: In a stand mixer, beat together the butter and sugar until light and fluffy. With the mixer running, beat in one egg, followed by one-quarter of the ground almonds. Repeat until all the eggs and almonds are incorporated and the frangipane is smooth.

6. Line a baking sheet with parchment paper. On a lightly floured work surface, roll out the dough into a 14-inch circle about ¼ inch thick. Transfer to the prepared baking sheet. Spread the frangipane in an even layer in the center of the circle, leaving 3 to 4 inches bare around the edge. Arrange the plum halves on top, cut-side down, so that they are touching but not overlapping. Fold the dough over the filling to create the top crust: starting at the bottom of the crust, fold a 3- or 4-inch section inward toward the filling, and then fold a section of the same size that slightly overlaps with your first fold (you can move to the left or right, it doesn't matter). The overlapping section will create a nice little pleat in the dough. Continue to make slightly overlapping folds all the way around the edge of the tart. Bake for 45 minutes, or until a knife inserted into the middle of the frangipane comes out clean.

7. Remove the pie from the oven. Reheat the plum glaze over low heat until it thins out, about 2 minutes, and use a pastry brush to paint it over the plums.

8. Scatter the toasted almonds over the top, and serve warm with a large scoop of vanilla ice cream or a dollop of whipped cream.

You can also make this pie in a dough-lined pie tin or a tart pan as pictured on page 73.

PEAR AND HONEYED GOAT CHEESE GALETTE

MAKES ONE
9-INCH PIE

I love goat cheese. I order it at restaurants whenever I can and add it to salads at home. While it's a common item in Los Angeles, it's still hard to find in grocery stores where I live in Pennsylvania. My love for it started with this pie, my goat-cheese gateway. It has the same salty-sweet combination of Apple-Cheddar Pie (page 46), a lifelong favorite of mine. So it's really no wonder I like it so much.

1. To make the goat cheese crust: In a large bowl, stir together the flour and salt. Add the butter and goat cheese, and use a pastry blender to cut them into the flour until the mixture is crumbly. Add the vinegar and stir until combined. Add the water, 1 tablespoon at a time, and mix just until the dough comes together into a ball. Turn the dough out onto a lightly floured counter, and shape into a disk. Wrap tightly in plastic wrap and refrigerate for at least 30 minutes.

2. Preheat the oven to 425°F. Line a baking sheet with parchment paper.

3. To make the honeyed goat cheese: In a medium bowl, whisk together the goat cheese and honey. Add the brown sugar and nutmeg and continue to whisk vigorously until the cheese is light and airy, about 3 minutes.

4. On the lightly floured work surface, roll out the dough into a 14-inch circle about ¼ inch thick. Transfer to the baking sheet. Spread the goat cheese filling onto the dough, leaving a 2-inch border. Set aside.

Goat Cheese Crust

2 cups all-purpose flour

1 teaspoon kosher salt

¾ cup cold salted butter, cubed

4 ounces cold goat cheese

1 tablespoon apple cider vinegar

2 tablespoons ice water

Honeyed Goat Cheese

6 ounces goat cheese, at room temperature

3 tablespoons clover honey

1½ tablespoons packed dark brown sugar

¼ teaspoon freshly grated nutmeg

3 ripe but firm pears, such as Bosc, Bartlett, or Red Anjou

1 egg

1 tablespoon water

1 tablespoon granulated sugar

Clover honey for garnish

1 sprig of fresh rosemary for garnish

continued ⟶

5. Cut the pears in half lengthwise through the stem ends, and scoop out the core of each half. Place the pears, cut-side down, on a cutting board. Leaving the top ½ inch below the stem end intact, thinly slice the pears. Fan the pears out and place on top of the filling, stem ends in the middle, overlapping the slices as needed. Fold the dough over the filling to create the top crust: starting at the bottom of the crust, fold a 3- or 4-inch section inward toward the filling, and then fold a section of the same size that slightly overlaps with your first fold (you can move to the left or right, it doesn't matter). The overlapping section will create a nice little pleat in the dough. Continue to make slightly overlapping folds all the way around the edge of the galette.

6. In a small bowl, whisk together the egg and water. Brush the egg wash over the dough, and sprinkle with the granulated sugar.

7. Bake for 25 to 35 minutes, or until the crust is golden. Garnish with a drizzle of honey and a sprig of rosemary laid over the center of the galette.

8. Serve warm, or cool on the counter until room temperature, about 2 hours.

ORANGE-GINGER RICOTTA PIE

Crust

1½ cups all-purpose flour

1 tablespoon chopped crystallized ginger

2 teaspoons sugar

½ cup salted butter

2 tablespoons ice water

Filling

One 8-ounce package cream cheese, at room temperature

¼ cup sugar

1 teaspoon vanilla extract

2 eggs

One 15-ounce package whole-milk ricotta cheese

¼ cup orange marmalade

1 teaspoon whole milk

¼ teaspoon kosher salt

Flavors really add up differently in a pie, depending on which component of the pie they live in. Sometimes an unexpected spice in the filling tastes like a bit of genius, such as in the Cardamom-Cherry Pie (page 85). In other pies, it's a topping or garnish that makes all the difference, like the espresso whipped cream served with Spiced Hot Chocolate Pie (page 131). In this pie, it's all about the crystallized ginger tucked into the crust, giving it a nice little chewy bite with a kick of heat. Give it a try and you'll see—the ginger just works there!

1. To make the crust: In a large mixing bowl, stir together the flour, ginger, and sugar. Using a pastry blender or your fingertips, work the butter into the flour mixture until it becomes pebbly, like coarse sand. Add the water, 1 tablespoon at a time, stirring it into the flour mixture until the dough begins to come together into a ball. Wrap in plastic wrap and chill for at least 1 hour.

2. Preheat the oven to 350°F.

3. Roll out the dough, and lay it in a 9-inch pie pan. Use the tines of a fork to poke holes in the bottom and sides, which will keep the crust from bubbling. Trim and flute the edge according to the instructions on page 23. Bake for 15 minutes, or until the crust is light golden brown. Set aside to cool.

4. Increase the oven temperature to 375°F.

5. To make the filling: In the bowl of a stand mixer fitted with the paddle attachment, beat the cream cheese and sugar on medium speed until fluffy, about 3 minutes. Add the vanilla and eggs and continue to mix until smooth. Add the ricotta, marmalade, milk, and salt, and mix until thoroughly combined.

6. Scoop the filling into the parbaked crust and bake for 20 to 25 minutes, or until the outer edges of the filling begin to puff and the center is no longer jiggly. Cool on the counter for 2 hours, and then cover and refrigerate for 8 hours, or until the filling is firm and completely chilled. Serve cold.

GOLD-DUSTED RASPBERRY AND CHAMPAGNE–CREAM CHEESE PIE

MAKES ONE 9-INCH PIE

Inspired by the Academy Awards, this pie is appropriately luxe. Not only does it have edible gold on the top, but it also includes sparkling wine in the mix. The bubbles feature both in the cream cheese–based filling and in the whipped cream slathered over the top.

1. Preheat the oven to 375°F

2. Roll out the crust, and lay it in a 9-inch pie pan. Use the tines of a fork to poke holes in the bottom and sides, which will keep the crust from bubbling. Trim and flute the edge according to the instructions on page 23. Bake for 35 to 40 minutes, or until golden brown. Set aside to cool completely.

3. To make the cream cheese filling: In a large bowl, use a handheld electric mixer on medium speed to beat the cream cheese, confectioners' sugar, and vanilla until smooth. With the mixer running, gradually add the cream, and continue beating until thickened. Spoon the cream cheese mixture into the fully baked piecrust and use a spatula to spread it out evenly.

4. To make the raspberry filling: In a large saucepan, combine the granulated sugar, cornstarch, and salt. Add the sparkling wine and whisk until smooth. Stir in 1 cup of the raspberries. Bring the mixture to a boil over medium-high heat and continue boiling for 1 minute, stirring constantly. Remove from the heat and cool completely, about 30 minutes. Add the remaining 1 cup raspberries to the cooled mixture, stirring gently to coat the berries with the sauce. Spoon the topping over the cream cheese layer of the pie, and refrigerate for at least 2 hours.

5. To make the raspberry whipped cream: In a medium bowl, combine the cream, granulated sugar, and sparkling wine. Beat with a handheld electric mixer on high until stiff peaks form.

6. Top the pie with a big mound of whipped cream, arrange the remaining raspberries, and dust the top with the edible gold glitter. Serve cold.

½ recipe Moe's Piecrust (page 19)

Cream Cheese Filling

1¾ cups cream cheese, at room temperature

½ cup confectioners' sugar

¼ teaspoon vanilla extract

⅔ cup heavy cream

Raspberry Filling

⅓ cup granulated sugar

1½ tablespoons cornstarch

⅛ teaspoon kosher salt

⅓ cup raspberry sparkling wine (I like Verdi Raspberry Sparkletini)

2 cups fresh raspberries, plus a handful for garnish

Raspberry Whipped Cream

1 cup heavy cream

1 tablespoon granulated sugar

1 tablespoon raspberry sparkling wine

Edible gold glitter for dusting the pie

VEGAN BLACKBERRY-MANGO GALETTE

There's no pie pan required for this recipe. The free-form galette is baked on a parchment-lined cookie sheet, and while in the oven, the blackberry juices run out of the crust, caramelizing on the parchment paper in a gooey mess. To me, that's a good sign, promising something wonderfully delicious.

Crust

2 cups all-purpose flour

⅓ cup organic cane sugar

½ teaspoon kosher salt

½ cup cold vegan butter (I like Country Crock plant butter)

2 to 3 tablespoons ice water

Filling

4 cups fresh blackberries

1½ teaspoons grated lemon zest

1 tablespoon plus 1 teaspoon freshly squeezed lemon juice

¼ to ½ cup granulated sugar, depending on sweetness of berries

1½ teaspoons cornstarch or arrowroot powder

1 cup pitted, peeled, and cubed mango (or thawed frozen mango)

Vegan vanilla ice cream for serving

1. Preheat the oven to 350°F. Line a baking sheet with parchment paper.

2. To make the crust: In a large bowl, combine the flour, cane sugar, and salt. Using a pastry blender, cut in the vegan butter until the mixture is crumbly. Add 1 tablespoon of the ice water and use a spoon to stir it into the mixture. With your hands, work the dough just enough so that it comes together, adding 1 or 2 more tablespoons of ice water if needed. Dump the dough onto the counter and press it out into a disk. Wrap it in plastic wrap and refrigerate.

3. To make the filling: In a large bowl, combine the berries, lemon zest and juice, granulated sugar, and cornstarch, and stir to combine.

4. On a floured surface, roll out the chilled dough into a 9-inch circle and transfer to the prepared baking sheet. Spread out the blackberry filling over the crust, leaving about a 1-inch border. Arrange the mango cubes over the blackberries. Fold the dough over the filling to create the top crust: starting at the bottom of the crust, fold a 3- or 4-inch section inward toward the filling, and then fold a section of the same size that slightly overlaps with your first fold (you can move to the left or right, it doesn't matter). The overlap will create a nice little pleat in the dough. Continue to make slightly overlapping folds all the way around the edge of the galette, leaving an open space in the middle of the galette. It doesn't have to be perfect.

5. Bake for 35 to 40 minutes, until the fruit is tender and bubbling. Serve warm with vegan vanilla ice cream.

CARDAMOM-CHERRY PIE

MAKES ONE 9-INCH PIE

This pie was created as an alternative to the holiday classics, like pumpkin and sweet potato, and it really shows how a familiar flavor can be changed completely with just a few small additions. The spices, driven by the cardamom, take the summery flavor of cherry and turn it into something more brooding and complex—perfect for the wintertime.

¾ cup packed dark brown sugar

2½ tablespoons cornstarch

½ teaspoon kosher salt

3 teaspoons ground cardamom

½ teaspoon freshly grated nutmeg

¼ teaspoon ground cloves

1 quart sour cherries, pitted

Moe's Piecrust (page 19)

1. Preheat the oven to 450°F.

2. In a small bowl, stir together the brown sugar, cornstarch, salt, cardamom, nutmeg, and cloves. Put the cherries in a large saucepan and add the spice mixture. Cook over medium-high heat. The cherries will release their juices and begin to thicken and bubble. When the juices become thick and the cherries collapse, remove from the heat, 8 to 10 minutes. Let cool.

3. Roll out the bottom and top crusts. Lay the bottom crust in a 9-inch pie pan. Fill with the cooked cherries, mounding the fruit up high in the middle. Make slits in the top crust and lay it over the filling. Pinch the edges of the two crusts together to seal, and flute according to the instructions on page 23. Or you can make a lattice top (see page 24).

4. Place the pie on a cookie sheet (to catch the drips) and bake for 10 minutes. Lower the heat to 350°F and bake for 25 minutes longer, or until the top is beginning to brown and the filling is bubbling up through the slits.

5. Serve the pie warm, or cool on the counter until room temperature, about 2 hours.

CHAPTER 3

meringue pies

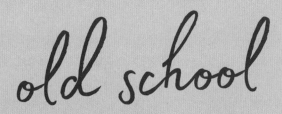

old school

I had a hard time getting the chefs at the Pie Hole to make a meringue pie. They had all sorts of complaints: It slides around, or the peaks are too high and don't fit in our refrigerators. Meringue, they seemed to be saying, was too finicky. Mentally, it's a lot like learning to make a piecrust. You may worry about succeeding, but after making it a few times, you will master it and enjoy the process, too.

Not all meringue pies are great. Often the meringue is a foamy, frothy thing, almost chewy. That's not what you want at all. The ideal texture is that of a fluffy cloud that almost dissolves when you bite into it.

While I don't like everyone's lemon meringue, I do like mine. The filling is soft and smooth and tastes of actual lemons. The meringue almost floats on top of the lemon layer. It doesn't hold a perfect shape when you cut it, but that's the sign of a good meringue pie.

There's one key to making a meringue pie work: your egg whites must be room temperature. If you use eggs straight out of the fridge, the meringue will weep. If you put your eggs on the counter ahead of time and allow them to warm up, you'll be able to get that big, beautiful cloud on the top.

The meringue should spread all the way to the edge of the crust. You don't want to see the lemon filling or whatever is underneath, because that lets out moisture. And you want to put the meringue on while the filling is still hot. Doing so will help you avoid a number of meringue-pie pitfalls: no skin will develop on the top of the filling, you'll have a better seal between the meringue and the edge of the crust (which prevents shrinking), and it helps avoid any weeping on top of the meringue, too. Finally, don't torch the meringue. That will cook just the outside, and the uncooked meringue will deflate. Instead, brown the meringue in the oven.

We don't put these pies on the menu at the shop all that often. Working on a large scale, as we do at the Pie Hole, things can go wrong, and we'll get a sweaty pie or a slipping pie. But a meringue is the perfect type of pie for the home baker to master. You're going to be making only one or two, and you can follow each step carefully. The result will be glorious and will convert anyone who tries your pie into a meringue lover.

I love the all-over golden color of a baked meringue-topped pie, as opposed to the uneven charred look of a torched one. Torches do have a place in the kitchen: for flaming the top of a crème brûlée, or to toast the marshmallows on a S'mores Pie (page 139). But in my kitchen, a torch is not going anywhere near my meringue pies.

LEMON MERINGUE PIE

½ recipe Moe's Piecrust
(page 19)

Filling

1½ cups sugar

3 tablespoons cornstarch

3 tablespoons all-purpose
flour

½ teaspoon kosher salt

1½ cups hot tap water

3 egg yolks

2 tablespoons salted butter

½ teaspoon grated
lemon zest

½ cup freshly squeezed
lemon juice

Meringue

3 egg whites, at room
temperature

½ teaspoon vanilla extract

¼ teaspoon cream of tartar

¼ cup plus 2 tablespoons
sugar

During the pie tastings we did before we opened the first shop, I was told by a number of people that they didn't even like lemon meringue pie, but that ours was the best thing that they had ever put in their mouths. I always got compliments from my family and my church family about my pies. But it was a real boost to hear that other people did not just like them—they really, *really* liked them.

1. Preheat the oven to 375°F.

2. Roll out the crust, and lay it in a 9-inch pie pan. Use the tines of a fork to poke holes in the bottom and sides, which will keep the crust from bubbling. Trim and flute the edge according to the instructions on page 23. Bake for 35 to 40 minutes, or until golden brown. Set aside to cool completely.

3. Lower the oven temperature to 350°F.

4. To make the filling: In a medium saucepan, stir together the sugar, cornstarch, flour, and salt. Gradually stir in the hot water and bring to a boil over high heat, stirring constantly. Lower the heat to medium, and cook, stirring, 2 minutes longer, or until the mixture is glossy and thick. Remove from the heat. In a small heatproof bowl, whisk together the egg yolks and slowly whisk in a ladleful of the sugar mixture to temper them. Pour the tempered yolks back into the hot sugar mixture, and bring to a boil over medium heat. Cook for 2 minutes longer, stirring constantly. Remove from the heat, and stir in the butter and lemon zest. Slowly add the lemon juice. Pour into the baked pie shell and set aside.

5. To make the meringue: In a large bowl, use an electric mixer on high speed to beat the egg whites, vanilla, and cream of tartar until soft peaks form. With the mixer running, gradually add the sugar, 1 tablespoon at a time, beating until stiff and glossy peaks form and the sugar is dissolved. If you haven't added all 6 tablespoons at this point, don't add any more (I rarely use all of the sugar). Spread the meringue over the hot filling, all the way to the edge of the piecrust. This will seal in the filling and prevent the meringue from shrinking.

6. Bake for 12 to 15 minutes, or until the meringue is golden. Cool completely on the counter, at least 4 hours, and refrigerate for 3 hours. Serve cold.

The trick to cutting a neat slice of meringue pie is a wet knife: first, dip the knife in water and use the wet blade to score the very top of the meringue. Then, cut down through the score marks all the way through the crust. The combination of a wet knife and the scoring prevents the knife from dragging the meringue across the filling.

CHOCOLATE ANGEL PIE

Unlike the fluffy meringue that goes on top of pies, this is a load-bearing meringue that contains a filling, in lieu of a piecrust. Despite being both delicious and a guaranteed conversation starter, angel pies like this one are a historic oddity of American pie baking, which most people have never heard of. But show one to a Francophile, like our CEO Sean, and their eyes will light up. French pastry chefs love their baked meringues, and this recipe brings that dry, crackly texture to the world of American pie. I've made this pie with the meringue crust baked in a pie pan, which gives it a well-defined shape. But I like the drama of piping out a free-form shell (see page 88), which results in a beautiful meringue cloud.

1. Preheat the oven to 275°F. Line a baking sheet with parchment paper.

2. To make the meringue shell: In a large bowl, use an electric mixer on high speed to beat the egg whites and cream of tartar until foamy. With the mixer running, add the sugar, 1 tablespoon at a time, until soft peaks form. When you lift the mixer out of the bowl, the egg whites should stand up briefly, and then the pointed top of the peak should gradually collapse. Scoop the meringue into a pastry bag fitted with the largest tip you have. Starting in the center of the baking sheet, pipe tight, concentric circles of meringue until you have about a 9-inch round. Pipe layers of meringue around the outer edge of the circle to create a rim. Don't be too precious about the process—it's free-form. You just want a relatively solid bottom and sides.

3. Bake the meringue for 50 minutes, or until firmly set and golden, with some small cracks showing. Slide the parchment and shell together onto a wire rack and cool for at least 4 hours.

4. Meanwhile, make the filling: In a double boiler or a heatproof bowl nestled into a saucepan with simmering water below, melt the chocolate chips. Pour in the coffee and stir until it is completely incorporated and the mixture is smooth. Remove from the heat and stir in the vanilla. Set aside to cool. In a medium bowl, use an electric mixer to whip the cream until it holds soft peaks. Gently fold the whipped cream into the chocolate mixture.

5. Pour the filling into the cooled meringue shell, and refrigerate for 4 hours. Serve cold.

Meringue Shell

2 egg whites, at room temperature

⅛ teaspoon cream of tartar

½ cup sugar

Filling

1 cup semisweet chocolate chips

3 tablespoons strong brewed coffee

1 teaspoon vanilla extract

1 cup heavy cream

PINEAPPLE MERINGUE PIE

½ recipe Moe's Piecrust
(page 19)

Filling

One 20-ounce can crushed pineapple (do not drain)

1 cup sour cream

¾ cup sugar

¼ cup all-purpose flour

1 tablespoon freshly squeezed lemon juice

½ teaspoon kosher salt

2 egg yolks

Meringue

3 egg whites, at room temperature

½ teaspoon vanilla extract

¼ teaspoon cream of tartar

¼ cup plus 2 tablespoons sugar

This recipe has an unusual distinction in this cookbook: it's the only one that calls exclusively for canned fruit. But while you could conceivably make it with fresh pineapple, this pie is a delicious relic of the 1950s and '60s, when there was practically an entire cuisine built around canned pineapple. Pineapple glazed ham, sweet-and-sour tuna with canned pineapple, Jell-O "salads" shot through with chunks of syrupy sweet pineapple. This pie comes from the same tradition, so don't bother with fresh fruit.

1. Preheat the oven to 375°F.

2. Roll out the crust, and lay it in a 9-inch pie pan. Use the tines of a fork to poke holes in the bottom and sides, which will keep the crust from bubbling. Trim and flute the edge according to the instructions on page 23. Bake for 35 to 40 minutes, or until golden brown. Set aside to cool completely.

3. Lower the oven temperature to 350°F.

4. To make the filling: In a large saucepan, combine the pineapple with its syrup, the sour cream, sugar, flour, lemon juice, and salt. Cook over medium heat until the mixture begins to bubble, and cook, stirring, for 2 minutes more. In a medium heatproof bowl, whisk together the egg yolks. Continue to whisk vigorously while adding a few splashes of the hot pineapple mixture into the bowl to temper the eggs. Dump everything back into the pan, and cook for 2 minutes longer, stirring constantly.

5. Pour the filling into the pie shell and set aside.

6. To make the meringue: In a large bowl, use an electric mixer on high speed to beat the egg whites, vanilla, and cream of tartar until soft peaks form. With the mixer running, gradually add the sugar, 1 tablespoon at a time, beating until stiff and glossy peaks form and the sugar is dissolved. If you haven't added all 6 tablespoons at this point, don't add any more (I rarely use all of the sugar). Spread the meringue over the hot filling, going all the way to the edge of the piecrust. This will seal in the filling and prevent the meringue from shrinking.

7. Bake for 12 to 15 minutes, or until the meringue is golden. Cool completely on the counter, at least 4 hours, and refrigerate for at least 3 hours. Serve cold.

PEANUT BUTTER CRUNCH PIE

My partner, Ben, and I have been together for six years, and I've known all along that he's a big peanut butter fan. But it was only on a recent trip to Los Angeles that he first tried this pie, which is now his favorite of all of the pies we make at the Pie Hole. It's the little bits of peanut butter crunchies shot through the filling that really put it over the top for him. I'm not sure why I had never made it for him before that trip, but I've made it for him plenty of times since then. It's a pie I've always enjoyed, too, but now it's even more near and dear to my heart.

1. Preheat the oven to 375°F.

2. Roll out the crust, and lay it in a 9-inch pie pan. Use the tines of a fork to poke holes in the bottom and sides, which will keep the crust from bubbling. Trim and flute the edge according to the instructions on page 23. Bake for 35 to 40 minutes, or until golden brown. Set aside to cool completely.

3. Lower the oven temperature to 350°F.

4. To make the crunchies: In a medium bowl, stir together the peanut butter and confectioners' sugar until well combined and crumbly. Reserve 2 tablespoons of the peanut butter crumbles to use for garnish. Sprinkle the rest over the bottom of the pie shell.

5. To make the filling: In a medium saucepan, whisk together the egg yolks and granulated sugar. Add the cornstarch, flour, salt, and milk, and bring to a boil over medium heat, stirring constantly. Cook, stirring, for 2 minutes. Remove from the heat and add the butter and vanilla. Stir until the butter melts and the mixture turns glossy. Pour over the peanut butter crunchies in the crust.

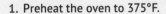

continued ⟶

½ recipe Moe's Piecrust (page 19)

Crunchies

½ cup crunchy peanut butter

⅔ cup confectioners' sugar

Filling

3 egg yolks

⅔ cup granulated sugar

3 tablespoons cornstarch

1 tablespoon all-purpose flour

½ teaspoon kosher salt

3 cups whole milk

2 tablespoons salted butter

1 teaspoon vanilla extract

Meringue

3 egg whites, at room temperature

¼ teaspoon cream of tartar

6 tablespoons granulated sugar

6. To make the meringue: In a large mixing bowl, use an electric mixer on high speed to beat the egg whites and cream of tartar until soft peaks form. With the mixer running, gradually add the granulated sugar, 1 tablespoon at a time, beating until stiff and glossy peaks form and the sugar is dissolved. If you haven't added all 6 tablespoons at this point, don't add any more (I rarely use all of the sugar). Spread the meringue over the hot filling, going all the way to the edge of the piecrust. This will seal in the filling and prevent the meringue from shrinking. Sprinkle the top with the reserved peanut butter crunchies.

7. Bake for 10 minutes, or until the meringue is light golden brown. Cool completely on the counter, at least 4 hours, and refrigerate for at least 3 hours. Serve cold.

Meringue is touchy, it's true. Like a toddler, there are just so many things that will make it weep! Weeping meringue still tastes good, but it does spoil the drama and beauty of a big golden cap on top of the pie. Room-temperature egg whites help, and so does letting the finished pie cool completely on the counter before you pop it in the fridge. If a meringue pie hits the refrigerator when it's still warm, the meringue is guaranteed to weep.

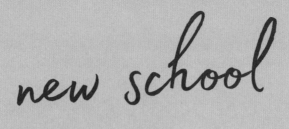

new school

Meringue pies are ripe for riffing on: the cooked filling flavored with lemon or pineapple in an old-school pie can readily take on new flavors. And a meringue topping can bring delight to just about any pie, no matter the flavor. So it's no wonder that the Pie Hole chefs have created a bunch of delightful new meringue pies. Most of the experimentation happens in the filling, but not all of it. A little touch of spice mixed into your egg whites can take the meringue in a whole different direction.

MAKES ONE
9-INCH PIE

CARDAMOM–LEMON MERINGUE PIE

½ recipe Moe's Piecrust
(page 19)

Filling

3 egg yolks

1¼ cups sugar

⅓ cup plus 1 tablespoon
cornstarch

1½ cups water

½ cup freshly squeezed
lemon juice

3 tablespoons salted butter

1 tablespoon grated
lemon zest

¼ teaspoon kosher salt

Meringue

3 egg whites, at room
temperature

½ teaspoon vanilla extract

¼ teaspoon cream of tartar

¼ cup plus 2 tablespoons
sugar

½ teaspoon ground
cardamom

Like the Cardamom-Cherry Pie (page 85), this is another old-school classic that gets a lovely contemporary gloss from an extra bit of spice. Cardamom is no stranger to bakers, but here its mellow flavor comes as a very pleasant surprise. Adding a touch to the meringue gives a bit of complexity to the sugar and fluff (not that there's anything wrong with that!), and it pairs with the lemon wonderfully. This is like the classic Lemon Meringue Pie (page 90) in a fancy new suit—familiar, but more sophisticated.

1. Preheat the oven to 375°F.

2. Roll out the crust, and lay it in a 9-inch pie pan. Use the tines of a fork to poke holes in the bottom and sides, which will keep the crust from bubbling. Trim and flute the edge according to the instructions on page 23. Bake for 35 to 40 minutes, or until golden brown. Set aside to cool completely.

3. Increase the oven temperature to 400°F.

4. To make the filling: In a medium heatproof bowl, whisk the egg yolks until smooth. In a medium saucepan, combine the sugar and cornstarch, and then gradually whisk in the water. Bring to a boil over medium heat, whisking constantly, and continue boiling, whisking constantly, for 1 minute, or until the mixture is very thick.

5. Whisking vigorously, slowly pour in half of the hot sugar mixture into the egg yolks to temper them. Whisk the egg yolks back into the pot and bring to a boil over medium heat, whisking constantly. Boil for 2 minutes, continuing to whisk constantly. Remove from the heat and stir in the lemon juice, butter, lemon zest, and salt. Pour into the prepared piecrust and set aside.

100   PIE IS MESSY

6. To make the meringue: In a large bowl, use an electric mixer to beat the egg whites, vanilla, and cream of tartar until soft peaks form. With the mixer running, gradually add the sugar, 1 tablespoon at a time, beating until stiff and glossy peaks form and the sugar is dissolved. If you haven't added all 6 tablespoons at this point, don't add any more (I rarely use all of the sugar). Beat in the cardamom.

7. Spread the meringue over the hot filling, going all the way to the edge of the piecrust. This will seal in the filling and prevent the meringue from shrinking. Bake for 12 to 15 minutes, or until the meringue is golden brown.

8. Cool completely on the counter, at least 4 hours, and refrigerate for at least 3 hours. Serve cold.

STRAWBERRY CREAM MERINGUE PIE

MAKES ONE 9-INCH PIE

A fluffy cap of meringue will give any dessert an ethereal look, and with its berry-pink filling hiding underneath, this pie is particularly dreamy. Even though it looks more like a kid's fantasy of dessert, it's one of my summertime favorites!

1. Preheat the oven to 375°F.

2. Roll out the crust, and lay it in a 9-inch pie pan. Trim and flute the edge according to the instructions on page 23. Bake for 35 to 40 minutes, or until golden brown. Set aside to cool completely. Lower the oven temperature to 350°F.

3. To make the filling: Hull and thinly slice the strawberries. Transfer to a medium saucepan and add the sugar, flour, lemon juice, and salt, and stir to combine. Let sit for 10 minutes, off the heat, to allow the strawberries to release their juices. Add the butter and cook the fruit over medium heat until the butter is melted. Remove from the heat.

4. In a medium heatproof bowl, whisk together the egg yolks and cream. Whisk some of the hot liquid from the berries into the egg yolks to temper them. Pour the tempered eggs into the saucepan and cook over medium heat, stirring constantly, until the mixture comes to a boil. Remove from the heat and let cool to lukewarm. Pour the filling into the piecrust and set aside.

5. To make the meringue: In a large mixing bowl, use an electric mixer on high speed to beat the egg whites, vanilla, and cream of tartar until soft peaks form. With the mixer running, gradually add the sugar, 1 tablespoon at a time, beating until stiff and glossy peaks form and the sugar is dissolved. If you haven't added all 6 tablespoons at this point, don't add any more (I rarely use all of the sugar). Spread the meringue over the top of the hot pie, going all the way to the edge of the piecrust. This will seal in the filling and prevent the meringue from shrinking.

6. Bake for 12 to 15 minutes, or until the meringue is golden. Cool completely on the counter, at least 4 hours, and refrigerate for at least 3 hours. Serve cold.

½ recipe Moe's Piecrust (page 19)

Filling

1 quart plus 1 pint fresh strawberries

1 cup sugar

¼ cup plus 2 tablespoons all-purpose flour

1 tablespoon freshly squeezed lemon juice

¼ teaspoon kosher salt

1 tablespoon salted butter

3 egg yolks

2 tablespoons heavy cream

Meringue

3 egg whites, at room temperature

½ teaspoon vanilla extract

¼ teaspoon cream of tartar

¼ cup plus 2 tablespoons sugar

RASPBERRY MERINGUE PIE WITH A CHOCOLATE CRUST

Chocolate Crust

20 cream-filled chocolate sandwich cookies (I like Oreos)

6 tablespoons salted butter, melted

Filling

1½ pints fresh raspberries

½ cup sugar

2 tablespoons freshly squeezed lemon juice

2 tablespoons water

2 egg yolks

2 tablespoons cornstarch

Pinch of kosher salt

1 tablespoon salted butter

Meringue

3 egg whites, at room temperature

½ teaspoon vanilla extract

¼ teaspoon cream of tartar

¼ cup plus 2 tablespoons sugar

There's a certain levity to many meringue pies. It's not just the pouf of whipped eggs and sugar on top, but the flavors that often feature in the filling, too. Creamy lemon with a candied cloud on top? It's pure sunshine. But that's not all that meringue can do. This pie is more brooding and serious, like a brunette to lemon meringue's blonde—it's meringue after dark. And as you'll see, that wonderfully sweet airiness of the meringue topping plays just as well with a richer flavor combination such as chocolate and raspberries.

1. Preheat the oven to 300°F.

2. To make the chocolate crust: In a food processor, pulverize the sandwich cookies, cream filling and all. You should have about 1½ cups. Add the butter, and pulse a few times to combine. You'll know the "dough" is done when it starts to clump together.

3. Transfer the cookie mixture to a 9-inch pie pan and use your fingertips to press it evenly over the bottom and up the sides of the pan. You want to make sure the thickness of the crust is uniform, particularly where the bottom meets the side. Bake for 10 minutes, and then remove the pan from the oven and use the back of a metal spoon to immediately reshape the crust. Set aside.

4. Increase the oven temperature to 350°F.

5. To make the filling: In a medium saucepan, combine the raspberries, sugar, lemon juice, and water, and bring to a boil over medium heat. Lower the heat and simmer for 5 minutes. Remove from the heat. In a medium heatproof bowl, whisk together the egg yolks and cornstarch. Whisk in a few splashes of the hot raspberry mixture to temper the egg yolks. Pour the tempered eggs into the pan and return the mixture to a boil, over medium heat, stirring constantly. Cook, stirring, for about 1 minute more, or until the filling starts to thicken. Add the salt and butter and cook, stirring gently, until smooth and creamy. Pour the filling into the prepared chocolate cookie crust and set aside.

continued ⟶

6. To make the meringue: In a large bowl, use an electric mixer on high speed to beat the egg whites, vanilla, and cream of tartar until soft peaks form. With the mixer running, gradually add the sugar, 1 tablespoon at a time, beating until stiff and glossy peaks form and the sugar is dissolved. If you haven't added all 6 tablespoons at this point, don't add any more (I rarely use all of the sugar). Spread the meringue over the hot filling, going all the way to the edge of the piecrust. This will seal in the filling and prevent the meringue from shrinking.

7. Bake for 12 to 15 minutes, or until the meringue is golden. Cool completely on the counter, at least 4 hours, and refrigerate for at least 3 hours. Serve cold.

APRICOT MERINGUE PIE

MAKES ONE
9-INCH PIE

You don't come across them much anymore, but dried-fruit pies were once nearly as common as fresh-fruit pies. Here a classic dried-apricot pie—the kind you might have been served in winter for dessert in a midwestern farmhouse a century ago—gets a new-school update, courtesy of a fluffy cap of meringue.

1. Preheat the oven to 375°F.

2. Roll out the crust, and lay it in a 9-inch pie pan. Use the tines of a fork to poke holes in the bottom and sides, which will keep the crust from bubbling. Trim and flute the edge according to the instructions on page 23. Bake for 35 to 40 minutes, or until golden brown. Set aside to cool completely. Lower the oven temperature to 350°F.

3. To make the filling: In a medium bowl, combine the sugar, cornstarch, and salt and set aside. In a large saucepan, bring the apricots and water to a boil. Lower the heat and simmer for 10 minutes, or until the apricots are softened. Stir the sugar mixture into the pan, and bring to a boil over medium heat. Turn down the heat to low and cook, stirring, for 3 minutes, or until thickened. Remove from the heat.

4. In a medium heatproof bowl, whisk the egg yolks and, whisking constantly, add a few splashes of the hot apricot mixture into the egg yolks to temper them. Pour the tempered eggs into the pan, and bring to a gentle boil, stirring constantly. Cook, stirring, for 1 minute longer, or until the filling looks glossy. Remove from the heat and stir in the butter. Pour the hot filling into the crust.

5. To make the meringue: In a large bowl, use an electric mixer on high speed to beat the egg whites, vanilla, and cream of tartar until soft peaks form. With the mixer running, gradually add the sugar, 1 tablespoon at a time, beating until stiff and glossy peaks form and the sugar is dissolved. If you haven't added all 6 tablespoons at this point, don't add any more (I rarely use all of the sugar). Spread the meringue evenly over the filling, going all the way to the edge of the piecrust. This will seal in the filling and prevent the meringue from shrinking.

6. Bake for 12 to 15 minutes, or until the meringue is golden brown. Cool completely on the counter, at least 4 hours, and refrigerate for at least 3 hours. Serve cold.

½ recipe Moe's Piecrust
(page 19)

Filling

2 cups sugar

3 tablespoons cornstarch

¼ teaspoon kosher salt

12 ounces dried apricots,
chopped

1½ cups water

4 egg yolks

2 tablespoons salted butter

Meringue

4 egg whites, at room
temperature

½ teaspoon vanilla extract

¼ teaspoon cream of tartar

¼ cup plus 2 tablespoons
sugar

CHAPTER 4

cream pies

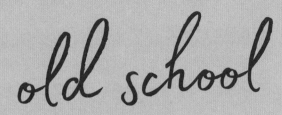

old school

When someone was coming over on short notice, when there was no fruit sitting around waiting to be made into a pie, when money was tight but something sweet and rich was called for, Moe would turn to cream pies. That's because dessert classics such as Chocolate Cream Pie (page 114), Banana Cream Pie (page 118), and Coconut Cream Pie (page 113) all share the same thrifty base: stove-top pudding made with milk, cornstarch, sugar, and eggs.

I remember watching my grandmother stir up a batch of the pudding in her kitchen, moving like she had four arms instead of two. She'd have a saucepan of milk and cornstarch warming up on the stove, dunking in a finger occasionally to feel if it was hot enough. At the same time, on the counter, she was separating the yolks and whites from eggs plucked straight from the chicken coops in the backyard, and mixing them together with sugar. The moment the milk felt right, she'd suddenly have a ladle in one hand and a fork in the other—never a whisk; I don't even think she owned one—and was quickly stirring the milk mixture into the eggs. All the while she also had meringue going for another couple of pies in another corner of the kitchen. She somehow managed to juggle it all perfectly (though gruffly).

The pudding Moe made, which you'll learn to replicate in this chapter, can be transformed into just about anything. Melt some chocolate into it and pour it into a graham cracker crust, just like my mom did every February for my brother Bob's birthday. Or dump it over a few sliced bananas. Even if you don't have a flock of laying hens to keep you in eggs, pudding pies are still quite easy (and cheap) to throw together. Pudding is what makes these pies feel like alchemy: you can make a rich, decadent dessert from almost nothing.

VANILLA CREAM PIE

**Graham Cracker Piecrust
(page 29)**

Filling

4 cups whole milk

2 tablespoons salted butter

4 egg yolks

1 cup sugar

¼ cup cornstarch

Pinch of kosher salt

2 teaspoons vanilla extract

Meringue

**4 egg whites, at room
temperature**

½ teaspoon vanilla extract

¼ teaspoon cream of tartar

**¼ cup plus 2 tablespoons
sugar**

This is as basic, and delicious, as it gets: cornstarch pudding flavored with vanilla, and topped with a cloud of meringue. The flavors may be subtle, but this recipe really shows just how much you can do with little more than eggs, sugar, and milk. If you don't want to bother with the meringue, you can top the pie with a mound of whipped cream instead (see My Favorite Whipped Cream recipe on page 45).

While a vanilla-flavored cream pie is wonderful in and of itself, this recipe functions as the blank canvas for nearly all of Moe's cornstarch-pudding pies. Add some sliced bananas, and you have a Banana Cream Pie (page 118). Stir in some Abuelita chocolate triangles and enjoy Spiced Hot Chocolate Pie (page 131). This is dessert, yes, but it's also a starting point.

1. Prepare and bake the graham cracker crust. Set aside. Keep the oven at 350°F.

2. To make the filling: In a saucepan, heat the milk and butter over low heat until the butter melts. In a medium heatproof bowl, whisk together the egg yolks, sugar, cornstarch, and salt. Whisk in a few splashes of the warm milk to temper the eggs, and then pour the mixture into the pan. Bring to a boil over medium heat, stirring constantly, and continue to boil, stirring, for 3 minutes. If you pull the pudding before it has cooked long enough, you'll end up with a soupy filling. The cornstarch needs enough heat and time to work. Remove the pan from the heat, and add the vanilla. Pour the filling into the cooled piecrust and set aside.

3. To make the meringue: In a large bowl, use an electric mixer on high speed to beat the egg whites, vanilla, and cream of tartar until soft peaks form. With the mixer running, gradually add the sugar, 1 tablespoon at a time, beating until stiff and glossy peaks form and the sugar is dissolved. If you haven't added all 6 tablespoons at this point, don't add any more (I rarely use all of the sugar). Spread the meringue over the hot filling, going all the way to the edge of the piecrust. This will seal in the filling and prevent the meringue from shrinking.

4. Bake for 12 to 15 minutes, or until the meringue is golden. Cool completely on the counter, at least 4 hours, and refrigerate for at least 3 hours. Serve cold.

COCONUT CREAM PIE

MAKES ONE 9-INCH PIE

I like this pie with whipped cream mounded over the top instead of meringue. Because you don't get the nice caramelized color of the baked meringue that way, I use a quick decorating trick: I take an extra bit of toasted coconut flakes and scatter them over the top of the whipped cream. I don't often garnish my pies, but it's an easy touch that looks very pretty.

½ recipe Moe's Piecrust (page 19)

Filling

4 cups whole milk

2 tablespoons salted butter

4 egg yolks

1 cup sugar

¼ cup cornstarch

Pinch of kosher salt

2 teaspoons vanilla extract

1⅓ cups coconut flakes

My Favorite Whipped Cream (page 45)

1. Preheat the oven to 375°F.

2. Roll out the crust, and lay it in a 9-inch pie pan. Use the tines of a fork to poke holes in the bottom and sides, which will keep the crust from bubbling. Trim and flute the edge according to the instructions on page 23. Bake for 35 to 40 minutes, or until golden brown. Set aside to cool completely.

3. To make the filling: In a saucepan, heat the milk and butter over low heat until the butter melts.

4. In a medium heatproof bowl, whisk together the egg yolks, sugar, cornstarch, and salt. Whisk in a few splashes of the warm milk to temper the eggs, and then pour the mixture into the pan. Bring to a boil over medium heat, stirring constantly, and continue to boil, stirring, for 3 minutes. Remove the pan from the heat, and stir in the vanilla and 1 cup of the coconut flakes. Pour the filling into the cooled piecrust, cover with plastic wrap, and cool for 2 hours on a wire rack. Move the pie to the refrigerator and chill for 2 hours more.

5. While the pie chills, toast the remaining coconut flakes: In a small nonstick pan, heat the remaining ⅓ cup coconut flakes over low heat, stirring frequently, until they turn toasty brown, 5 to 7 minutes.

6. Before serving, mound the whipped cream over the filling, and scatter the toasted coconut over the top.

CHOCOLATE CREAM PIE

**Graham Cracker Piecrust
(page 29)**

Filling

4 cups whole milk

2 tablespoons salted butter

**3 ounces unsweetened
chocolate, chopped**

4 egg yolks

1 cup sugar

¼ cup cornstarch

Pinch of kosher salt

2 teaspoons vanilla extract

Meringue

**4 egg whites, at room
temperature**

½ teaspoon vanilla extract

¼ teaspoon cream of tartar

**¼ cup plus 2 tablespoons
sugar**

It may not surprise you that ours was often a birthday pie house. My mom baked lovely cakes—she liked to make a chocolaty Wacky Cake, a delicious Depression-era innovation made with no butter or eggs, because we all loved chocolate so much. But more often than not a birthday was a day to pick a favorite pie for dessert. My older brother, Bob, whose birthday is in February, always chose this pie, made with a graham cracker crust and a fluffy cap of meringue on top. He always loved this pie, and it's a good thing, too, because February is in the fruit pie doldrums. Deep winter is when pantry-friendly cream pies like this reign supreme. Everything is probably already on hand, and you can whip up a celebratory pie out of very few ingredients. Bob passed away in 2011, and I still miss him very much. Whenever I make this pie for someone, in my heart I am making it for him.

1. Prepare and bake the graham cracker crust. Set aside. Keep the oven at 350°F.

2. To make the filling: In a medium saucepan, heat the milk, butter, and chocolate over low heat until the butter and chocolate melt. Stir until smooth. In a medium heatproof bowl, whisk together the egg yolks, sugar, cornstarch, and salt. Whisk in a few splashes of the warm milk mixture to temper the eggs, and then pour the mixture into the pan. Bring to a boil over medium heat, stirring constantly, and continue to boil, stirring, for 3 minutes. Remove the pan from the heat, and add the vanilla. Pour the filling into the cooled piecrust and set aside.

3. To make the meringue: In a large bowl, use an electric mixer on high speed to beat the egg whites, vanilla, and cream of tartar until soft peaks form. With the mixer running, gradually add the sugar, 1 tablespoon at a time, beating until stiff and glossy peaks form and the sugar is dissolved. If you haven't added all 6 tablespoons at this point, don't add any more (I rarely use all of the sugar). Spread the meringue over the hot filling, going all the way to the edge of the piecrust. This will seal in the filling and prevent the meringue from shrinking.

4. Bake for 12 to 15 minutes, or until the meringue is golden. Cool completely on the counter, at least 4 hours, and refrigerate for at least 3 hours. Serve cold.

BLUEBERRY CREAM PIE

You need a whole lot of fruit to make a double-crust blueberry pie. But for those times when you have little more than a pint and you're hankering for pie, this is the recipe to turn to. Instead of the usual cornstarch pudding cooked on the stove top, it's made with a sour cream–based filling that gives it an extra bit of tartness.

½ recipe Moe's Piecrust
(page 19)

Filling

1 cup sour cream

¾ cup sugar

2 tablespoons all-purpose
flour

1 teaspoon vanilla extract

¼ teaspoon kosher salt

1 egg

2½ cups fresh blueberries

1. Preheat the oven to 400°F.

2. Roll out the crust, and lay it in a 9-inch pie pan. Use the tines of a fork to poke holes in the bottom and sides, which will keep the crust from bubbling. Trim and flute the edge according to the instructions on page 23. Set aside.

3. To make the filling: In a medium bowl, with an electric mixer on medium speed, combine the sour cream, sugar, flour, vanilla, salt, and egg, and beat until smooth, about 5 minutes. Fold in the blueberries. Pour into the pie shell and bake for 25 minutes, or until the filling looks set and the top is just starting to brown.

4. While the pie bakes, make the topping: In a small bowl, combine the butter, nuts, and flour, and mash with a fork until well blended. Sprinkle the topping evenly over the pie, and bake for 10 minutes more, or until the topping is browned.

5. Refrigerate for at least 4 hours, and serve cold.

Topping

1½ tablespoons cold
salted butter, cubed

3 tablespoons chopped
walnuts or pecans

3 tablespoons all-purpose
flour

½ recipe Moe's Piecrust
(page 19)

Filling

4 cups whole milk

2 tablespoons salted butter

4 egg yolks

1 cup sugar

¼ cup cornstarch

Pinch of kosher salt

2 teaspoons vanilla extract

3 bananas, sliced

Meringue

4 egg whites, at room
temperature

½ teaspoon vanilla extract

¼ teaspoon cream of tartar

¼ cup plus 2 tablespoons
sugar

BANANA CREAM PIE

This is another one of those small tweak–big change recipes. It's Vanilla Cream Pie (page 112), with the addition of sliced bananas tucked underneath the filling. Just a simple, small addition that makes a world of difference in the flavor and feeling of the finished product. There's something so homey about this pie.

The bananas do brown rather quickly, and while that doesn't affect the taste of the pie, it doesn't look as nice when you slice into it. So this pie is best enjoyed on the same day it's made.

1. Preheat the oven to 375°F. Roll out the crust, and lay it in a 9-inch pie pan. Use the tines of a fork to poke holes in the bottom and sides, which will keep the crust from bubbling. Trim and flute the edge according to the instructions on page 23. Bake for 35 to 40 minutes, or until golden brown. Set aside to cool completely.

2. Lower the oven temperature to 350°F.

3. To make the filling: In a large saucepan, heat the milk and butter over low heat until the butter melts. In a medium heatproof bowl, whisk together the egg yolks, sugar, cornstarch, and salt. Whisk in a few splashes of the warm milk to temper the eggs, and then pour the mixture into the pan. Bring to a boil over medium heat, stirring constantly, and continue to boil, stirring for 3 minutes. Remove the pan from the heat, and add the vanilla. Place the sliced bananas over the bottom of the baked pie shell, and pour the filling over the bananas. Set aside.

4. To make the meringue: In a large bowl, use an electric mixer on high speed to beat the egg whites, vanilla, and cream of tartar until soft peaks form. With the mixer running, gradually add the sugar, 1 tablespoon at a time, beating until stiff and glossy peaks form and the sugar is dissolved. If you haven't added all 6 tablespoons at this point, don't add any more (I rarely use all of the sugar). Spread the meringue over the hot filling, going all the way to the edge of the piecrust. This will seal in the filling and prevent the meringue from shrinking.

5. Bake for 12 to 15 minutes, or until the meringue is golden. Cool completely on the counter, at least 4 hours, and refrigerate for at least 3 hours. Serve cold.

In my experience, the question of how long a pie will last has more to do with how quickly people will eat it, rather than how long it will actually be good to eat after sitting in the fridge or on the counter. But if you do have leftover pie, it will generally keep for at least 3 days in the fridge, covered with plastic wrap. The major exception to the 3-day rule is Banana Cream Pie, which should be eaten the same day it's made.

CHOCOLATE SILK PIE

The filling in this silky pie involves a lot of whisking and beating—beginning in a double boiler and finishing in a stand mixer—to make it very light and creamy. The resulting filling resembles a French custard, made luxurious with eggs and a fair bit of elbow grease.

**Graham Cracker Piecrust
(page 29)**

**3 ounces unsweetened
chocolate, chopped**

4 eggs

¾ cup sugar

2 tablespoons water

**½ cup plus 2 tablespoons
salted butter, at room
temperature**

¼ teaspoon kosher salt

**1½ teaspoons vanilla
extract**

**My Favorite Whipped
Cream (page 45)**

**Chocolate shavings
for garnish**

1. Prepare and bake the graham cracker crust. Set aside.

2. In a double boiler or a heatproof bowl nestled into a saucepan with simmering water below, warm the chocolate over medium heat until completely melted, 6 to 7 minutes. Remove from the heat, and scrape the chocolate into a small bowl. Wash and dry the top of the double boiler. Add the eggs, ½ cup of the sugar, and the water, and whisk to combine. Place the double boiler over medium heat and continue whisking until the eggs become thick and fluffy, and a drizzle of the mixture will hold its shape, about 5 minutes. Remove from the heat and set aside to cool, whisking occasionally so the eggs do not scramble.

3. In the bowl of a stand mixer, combine the butter, salt, and the remaining ¼ cup sugar and beat on medium-high speed until fluffy. Pour in the melted chocolate and vanilla and continue to beat, scraping down the sides of the bowl as needed, until well combined. Add the custard and beat until the filling is thick, fluffy, and smooth, about 5 minutes.

4. Spoon the filling into the piecrust and cover with plastic wrap. Refrigerate until chilled, 2 to 3 hours. Before serving, spread the whipped cream over the filling and garnish with the chocolate shavings.

MISSISSIPPI MUD PIE

½ recipe Moe's Piecrust
(page 19)

¾ cup sugar

3½ tablespoons cornstarch

⅛ teaspoon kosher salt

2½ cups whole milk

4 egg yolks

2 tablespoons salted butter

2 teaspoons vanilla extract

3 ounces unsweetened
chocolate, chopped

My Favorite Whipped
Cream (page 45)

½ cup mini–semisweet
chocolate chips

When we first opened the Pie Hole in L.A.'s Arts District, we got a lot of requests for various classic pies, including from quite a few people who came in asking if we could make a Mississippi mud pie. The thing about pie is that so much of it is regional, and when one of our team members, a born-and-bred Angeleno, heard someone asking for mud pie, she at first assumed that it was a joke. Were they talking about what kids made after it rained? Eventually, we figured out the disconnect, and put this pie on the menu.

1. Preheat the oven to 375°F.

2. Roll out the crust, and lay it in a 9-inch pie pan. Use the tines of a fork to poke holes in the bottom and sides, which will keep the crust from bubbling. Trim and flute the edge according to the instructions on page 23. Bake for 35 to 40 minutes, or until golden brown. Set aside to cool completely.

3. In a medium saucepan, whisk together the sugar, cornstarch, and salt. Add the milk and egg yolks, whisking until combined. Place the mixture over medium heat and whisk constantly until bubbles begin to form and the mixture begins to thicken. Add the butter, 1 tablespoon at a time, while continuing to whisk. Add the vanilla, and then gradually add the unsweetened chocolate, while still whisking, letting each bit melt into the mixture before adding more. Keep whisking over the heat until the mixture is smooth, thick, and glossy, about 4 minutes.

4. Pour the chocolate filling into the pie shell. Cover the pie with plastic wrap and refrigerate until cool, at least 1 hour. To finish the pie, cover the filling with a layer of whipped cream, mounding it high in the middle, and sprinkle the top with the mini–chocolate chips. Serve cold.

STRAWBERRY CHIFFON PIE

This pie is downright pretty—a dressed-up, fluffy pink cloud floating in a pie shell. The big layered mound of berry chiffon and whipped cream looks very impressive, but it's actually quite easy to make. The most difficult thing, really, is having enough patience to let the filling chill adequately, both before and after filling the pie. But as long as you have enough time on your hands, this is a low-effort, high-reward pie to bring with you to a family event or church function. It's always bound to impress.

1. Preheat the oven to 375°F.

2. Roll out the crust, and lay it in a 9-inch pie pan. Use the tines of a fork to poke holes in the bottom and sides, which will keep the crust from bubbling. Trim and flute the edge according to the instructions on page 23. Bake for 35 to 40 minutes, or until golden brown. Set aside to cool completely.

3. In a large bowl, use a potato masher to break up the strawberries until they are completely crushed. Stir in ½ cup of the sugar and let stand for 30 minutes. While the berry mixture sits, combine the gelatin and water in a small saucepan and dissolve the gelatin over low heat (don't allow the water to boil). Set aside to cool.

4. Add the gelatin, lemon juice, and salt to the strawberries, stirring to combine. Refrigerate until partially set, 8 to 10 minutes.

5. In a medium bowl, use an electric mixer to whip the cream until soft peaks form and set aside. In a large bowl, with clean beaters, beat the egg whites until soft peaks form. With the mixer running, gradually add the remaining ¼ cup sugar, beating until stiff and glossy peaks form and the sugar is dissolved.

6. Fold the strawberry mixture into the egg whites, and then fold in the whipped cream. Refrigerate until the filling holds its shape when you scoop up a bit with a spoon, almost like a scoop of ice cream, about 1 hour. Pile the filling into the pie shell and refrigerate until firm, about 5 hours. Top with My Favorite Whipped Cream before serving.

½ recipe Moe's Piecrust (page 19)

1 pint fresh strawberries, hulled

¾ cup sugar

1 tablespoon gelatin (1 envelope)

¾ cup cold water

1 tablespoon freshly squeezed lemon juice

Pinch of kosher salt

½ cup heavy cream

2 egg whites, at room temperature

My Favorite Whipped Cream (optional; page 45)

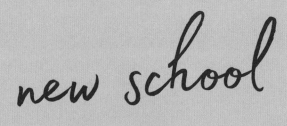

new school

In 2011, it seemed like all of Los Angeles was getting caught up in the upstairs-downstairs drama of *Downton Abbey,* even if the damp, gray English countryside felt like a world apart from Southern California. As the show's popularity grew, and the kitchen staff of the Pie Hole began talking about having a watch party, the chefs had an idea: What if we came up with a pie based on the show that people could eat while they watched? Among all of my family recipes, there isn't one that is based on a television show. Really, there isn't anything that even approaches a concept pie. This would be something completely new!

A number of ideas were batted around, but Beth Kellerhals, who was the executive chef at the time, came up with the winner, which became one of the Pie Hole's signature recipes. Her idea was to take the cream pie base of Moe's cornstarch puddings and flavor the filling with Earl Grey tea. I'll admit that I was skeptical. I didn't think you could make a pie by steeping tea bags, though it was a cute idea, and I liked its connection to *Downton Abbey.* But when I finally tasted the pie, I was immediately struck by the complexity of its layers. Altogether the tea, the chocolate, and the pistachios on top produced a total burst of flavor.

When it comes to new-school pies like the Earl Grey Pie (page 128), my job starts at the "taste this for me" phase, which is just the best kind of work. We don't really do sit-down, formal tastings of new pies; oftentimes, it's a very casual moment, like when I walk into the shop and get a slice plunked down in front of me with the question, "What do you think, Becky?" The blank-canvas quality of cream pies makes it easy to add layers of new flavor. Although Moe's cornstarch pudding is often the beginning, these recipes are infused with an array of ingredients that she would never have imagined in a pie: a variety of teas, cinnamon-spiced hot chocolate, and even breakfast cereal.

THE EARL GREY PIE

½ recipe Moe's Piecrust
(page 19)

Ganache

¾ cup heavy cream

1 Earl Grey tea bag
(I like Twinings)

½ cup semisweet chocolate
chips

1 tablespoon light corn syrup

2 tablespoons salted butter

Earl Grey Mousse

1½ cups heavy cream

½ cup whole milk

⅛ teaspoon kosher salt

1 tablespoon granulated
sugar

5 Earl Grey tea bags

1 tablespoon gelatin
(1 envelope)

¼ cup cold water

½ cup white chocolate,
coarsely chopped

¼ cup confectioners' sugar

⅛ teaspoon kosher salt

2 tablespoons chopped
unsalted pistachios

Pinch of kosher salt

My Favorite Whipped Cream
(page 45)

There's no denying it: This recipe has a lot of steps, probably more than any other in the book. But while it is involved, nothing is too, too difficult. What takes time is making the tea-infused cream for both the ganache and the white chocolate mousse. And letting those bags steep is what sets this pie apart from any others you've tasted. Which is to say, it's worth the extra effort.

1. Preheat the oven to 375°F.

2. Roll out the crust, and lay it in a 9-inch pie pan. Use the tines of a fork to poke holes in the bottom and sides, which will keep the crust from bubbling. Trim and flute the edge according to the instructions on page 23. Bake for 35 to 40 minutes, or until golden brown. Set aside to cool completely.

3. To make the ganache: In a small saucepan, combine the cream and tea bag, and heat over medium heat until the cream starts to bubble. Remove from the heat and steep the tea bag in the cream for 30 minutes. Remove the tea bag, pressing out any liquid into the pan, and set aside. In a large bowl, stir together the chocolate chips and corn syrup and set aside. In a small saucepan, combine the tea-infused cream and the butter, and heat over medium heat, stirring often, until the butter is melted. Pour over the chocolate chip mixture and whisk until the chocolate is completely melted. Set aside.

4. To make the Earl Grey mousse: In a small saucepan, combine ½ cup of the cream, the milk, salt, granulated sugar, and tea bags, and heat over medium heat until the liquid starts to bubble. Remove from the heat and steep the tea bags in the liquid for 30 minutes. Remove the tea bags, pressing out any additional liquid into the pan.

5. While the cream and tea mixture cools, dissolve the gelatin: In a small heatproof bowl, stir the gelatin into the water. Let sit for 5 minutes, and then stir again. Set the bowl of gelatin water inside a larger heatproof bowl, and fill that bowl with enough boiling water to come halfway up the side of the smaller bowl. Stir the gelatin until it dissolves completely. Put the white chocolate in a large heatproof bowl and set aside. Return the infused cream mixture to the stove, and stir in the confectioners' sugar and salt. Heat over medium heat until bubbles just begin to

continued ⟶

appear around the edges, and then whisk in the gelatin water. Pour the hot cream mixture over the white chocolate and whisk until the white chocolate melts completely. Cool, whisking occasionally to avoid any lumps.

6. In a large bowl, use an electric mixer to whip the remaining 1 cup cream until soft peaks form. After the white chocolate mixture has cooled, gradually and gently fold in the whipped cream, one-third at a time. Be careful not to overwork the mousse: if you stir it too vigorously or too much, it will lose its volume. Set aside.

7. Finally, assemble the pie: Spread out the ganache in an even layer over the bottom of the piecrust. Sprinkle with 1 tablespoon of the pistachios and the salt. Refrigerate for 30 minutes to set the ganache. Spoon the mousse over the ganache and spread it out evenly, filling the shell all the way to the edge of the crust. Scoop My Favorite Whipped Cream over the mousse and spread it out in an even layer, leaving a ½-inch border of mousse peeking out along the edge of the crust. Sprinkle the remaining 1 tablespoon pistachios over the whipped cream, and refrigerate for at least 4 hours. Serve cold.

SPICED HOT CHOCOLATE PIE

We originally made this pie for the very first tasting we had for family and friends before the first Pie Hole opened in the L.A. Arts District. A Mexican restaurant heard we were going to open a pie shop, and asked us to consider developing a pie for them. So we got to thinking: How could we incorporate Mexican flavors and ingredients into a pie? That collaboration ultimately never happened, but we got our wonderful spiced chocolate pie.

The idea of using cinnamon-flavored chocolate came from my son, Matty, who once worked at a car salvage yard. Most of the guys were Mexican American, and they would sometimes make a cup of hot chocolate at work. They made it for him once, and he loved the cinnamon flavor. That memory later sparked the idea for the pie.

At the bakery, the filling is made with a chocolate ganache flavored with pasilla peppers and cinnamon, but I like the original version we created for the restaurant: The base is a vanilla cornstarch pudding, flavored with cinnamon-spiced chocolate.

1. Preheat the oven to 375°F.

2. Roll out the crust, and lay it in a 9-inch pie pan. Use the tines of a fork to poke holes in the bottom and sides, which will keep the crust from bubbling. Trim and flute the edge according to the instructions on page 23. Bake for 35 to 40 minutes, or until golden brown. Set aside to cool completely.

3. To make the filling: In a saucepan, warm the milk and butter over medium heat until the butter melts. In a medium heatproof bowl, whisk the egg yolks, granulated sugar, cornstarch, and salt. Whisk in a few splashes of the warm milk to temper the eggs, and then pour the mixture into the pan. Bring to a boil over medium heat, stirring constantly, and continue to boil, stirring, for 2 minutes, or until the pudding thickens. Remove from the heat and add the vanilla and chocolate, stirring until the chocolate is melted, about 2 minutes.

½ recipe Moe's Piecrust
(page 19)

Filling

4 cups whole milk

2 tablespoons salted butter

4 egg yolks

1 cup granulated sugar

¼ cup cornstarch

Pinch of kosher salt

2 teaspoons vanilla extract

3 ounces Abuelita
brand chocolate
(about 2½ triangles)

Espresso Whipped Cream

1 cup heavy cream

3 tablespoons
confectioners' sugar

½ teaspoon vanilla extract

1 teaspoon instant
espresso

Chocolate curls for garnish
(optional; see page 152)

continued ⟶

4. Pour the pudding into the cooled piecrust, and cool on a wire rack for 2 hours and then refrigerate for at least 2 hours more.

5. To make the espresso whipped cream: In a medium metal mixing bowl, use an electric mixer on medium speed to beat the cream until it starts to thicken. Increase the speed to medium-high and continue to beat until the cream holds soft peaks. Add the confectioners' sugar, vanilla, and espresso powder, and continue to beat until stiff, but not grainy.

6. Serve each slice with a dollop of the whipped cream.

STRAWBERRY MOUSSE WITH CHOCOLATE-COVERED STRAWBERRIES

MAKES ONE 9-INCH PIE

They say you eat with your eyes first, and that certainly seems to be the case when we have one of these pies on display at the Pie Hole. The sight of the chocolate-covered strawberries nestled into the pretty pink mousse really draws people in. And how could it not? It makes you think of champagne and flickering candles, a romance in the form of a pie. And that, of course, makes it the perfect pie to bring on a date.

1. Prepare and bake the graham cracker crust. Set aside. Raise the oven temperature to 375°F.

2. To make the chocolate-covered strawberries: In a double boiler or a heatproof bowl nestled into a saucepan with simmering water below, melt the chocolate chips, stirring occasionally. Remove the pan from the heat, and remove the top of the double boiler from the pan. One by one, hold each strawberry by the hull and dunk the bottom two-thirds into the chocolate. Set on a sheet of wax paper and cool completely, at least 1 hour, before handling.

3. To make the strawberry preserves: In a medium saucepan, combine the strawberries with the sugar. Heat over medium-high heat, stirring constantly, as the warming sugar draws out the liquid from the berries. Increase the heat to high and boil, stirring occasionally, for 10 minutes. As the liquid reduces, the strawberry pieces will break down some, and the bubbles in the liquid will become more glossy and defined. Stir in the cornstarch and continue boiling for 3 minutes more, or until the mixture looks thickened. Set aside to cool. You should have about ¾ cup strawberry preserves.

½ recipe Graham Cracker Piecrust (page 29)

Chocolate-Covered Strawberries

1 cup semisweet chocolate chips

8 whole fresh strawberries

Strawberry Preserves

1½ cups chopped fresh strawberries

¾ cup sugar

1 tablespoon cornstarch

Mousse

1½ teaspoons gelatin (½ envelope)

¼ cup cold water

9 ounces white chocolate, coarsely chopped or white chocolate chips

½ cup whole milk

1½ cups heavy cream

¼ cup sugar

¼ teaspoon kosher salt

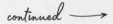

continued ⟶

4. To make the mousse: In a small heatproof bowl, stir the gelatin into the cold water. Let sit for 5 minutes, and then stir again. Set the small bowl of gelatin water inside a larger heatproof bowl, and fill that bowl with enough boiling water to come halfway up the side of the smaller bowl. Stir the gelatin until it dissolves completely.

5. Put the white chocolate in a large heatproof bowl. In a small saucepan, heat the milk and ¾ cup of the cream over medium heat. Add the sugar, salt, and strawberry preserves, and stir to combine. Heat until bubbles just begin to appear around the edges, and then whisk in the gelatin water. Pour the hot cream mixture over the white chocolate and whisk until the white chocolate melts completely. Cool, whisking occasionally to avoid any lumps.

6. In a large bowl, use an electric mixer to whip the remaining ¾ cup cream until soft peaks form. Gently fold half of the whipped cream into the mousse, and then fold in the remaining whipped cream, one-third at a time. Be careful not to overwork the mousse: if you stir it too vigorously or too much, it will lose its volume.

7. Spoon the mousse into the pie shell, and garnish with the chocolate-covered strawberries. Refrigerate until completely chilled, at least 4 hours. Serve cold.

S'MORES PIE

When my grandson, Jordan, was younger (he's twenty now), he was a Cub Scout. His troop often went on camping trips in the woods, which invariably included roasting marshmallows over a fire. The marshmallows gave him the idea of making this pie when he visited me one time—he liked to come up with ideas for pies during our visits. Originally, we made a chocolate pudding pie with a graham cracker crust, and topped it with torched marshmallows instead of meringue, and put it on the menu as a special that day: Jordan's Campfire S'mores Pie. And it sold out! He was very proud.

The pie has been modified a bit over the years. We use Marshmallow Fluff instead of individual marshmallows, and spread it across the bottom layer, because the pie is easier to slice that way. It does end up getting covered by chocolate mousse, but we toast the fluff with a torch, to give it a bit of that campfire taste. If you don't have a kitchen torch, you can run it under a broiler or just leave the fluff as is.

Graham Cracker Piecrust
(page 29)

1½ cups heavy cream

¼ cup sugar

2 teaspoons agar agar
powder (see page 140)

9 ounces semisweet
chocolate, coarsely
chopped

1¼ cups Marshmallow Fluff

My Favorite Whipped
Cream (page 45)

1 graham cracker, crumbled

¼ cup packaged semisweet
chocolate chunks

1. Prepare and bake the graham cracker crust. Set aside.

2. In a medium saucepan, combine ¾ cup of the cream, the sugar, and agar agar, and bring to a boil over medium heat, stirring constantly. Cook for 5 minutes, or until the mixture is thick and no longer grainy. Remove from the heat and pour into a large heatproof bowl. Stir in the chopped chocolate and cover with plastic wrap. Let sit for 10 minutes, allowing the cream to melt the chocolate.

3. Meanwhile, in a medium bowl, use an electric mixer to whip the remaining ¾ cup cream until it holds soft peaks. Uncover the chocolate and stir until it is completely melted and the mixture is smooth and glossy. Gently fold in the whipped cream, one-third at a time. Be careful not to overwork the mousse: if you stir it too vigorously or too much, it will lose its volume. Set aside.

continued ⟶

4. Spread out the Marshmallow Fluff in an even layer over the bottom of the piecrust, and brown the surface using a kitchen torch. Alternatively, you can brown the fluff under the broiler. Place the oven rack at least 6 inches away from the heat. Broil on high for 3 minutes, or until golden brown, checking frequently. If you used a broiler, allow the fluff and crust to cool completely before continuing.

5. Scoop the chocolate mousse over the toasted fluff, spreading it out into an even layer. Cover the mousse layer with My Favorite Whipped Cream, spreading it out from the center and leaving a ½-inch border of chocolate showing. Scatter the crumbled graham cracker and chocolate chunks over the top, and refrigerate for at least 4 hours. Serve cold.

The only thing you really need to know about agar agar is that it's an alternative to gelatin. It behaves a little differently—gelatin needs only to be warmed in order to thicken, while agar agar must be brought to a boil—but the end result is basically the same. The reason why a lot of the Pie Hole recipes are thickened with agar agar is because of how it's made: gelatin is an animal by-product, extracted from skin and bones, while agar agar is made from a type of seaweed. In order to keep these pies vegetarian, the chefs opt to use agar agar in many fillings. It's usually stocked at co-ops and health food stores, where it might be found in the Asian foods aisle.

MATCHA TEA PIE

After the Earl Grey Pie (page 128) came together, it was open season on tea pies in the Pie Hole kitchen. Using the same basic method of making a mousse with tea-infused cream, we could try anything! There were quite a few experiments hanging out on the counter, each with its own large plastic container full of cream and a raft of tea bags. Not everything made its way onto the menu, but a few were definite keepers, like this matcha pie. Not only does it have a lovely green filling, but it also gets slathered with whipped cream and drizzled with homemade caramel sauce before serving.

1. Preheat the oven to 375°F. Roll out the crust, and lay it in a 9-inch pie pan. Use the tines of a fork to poke holes in the bottom and sides, which will keep the crust from bubbling. Trim and flute the edge according to the instructions on page 23. Bake for 35 to 40 minutes, or until golden brown. Set aside to cool completely.

2. To make the mousse: In a small saucepan, heat the milk and ¾ cup of the cream over medium heat until bubbles start to form at the edge of the pan, and the liquid begins to give off steam. Transfer the scalded cream to a blender, add the matcha, and blend on low speed for 1 to 2 minutes, or until the matcha is fully incorporated, with no clumps remaining.

3. In a medium saucepan, combine the matcha cream, sugar, and agar agar, and bring to a boil over medium heat, stirring constantly. Cook, stirring, for 5 minutes, or until the mixture is thick and no longer grainy. Remove from the heat and transfer to a large heatproof bowl.

4. Add the white chocolate to the thickened matcha mixture, cover with plastic wrap, and let sit for 10 minutes, allowing the tea mixture to melt the white chocolate. Meanwhile, in a medium bowl, use an electric mixer to whip the remaining ¾ cup cream until it holds soft peaks. Uncover the matcha and white chocolate and stir until the white chocolate is completely melted and the mixture is smooth and glossy. Gently fold in the whipped cream, one-third at a time. Be careful not to overwork the mousse: if you stir it too vigorously or too much, it will lose its volume. Scoop the filling into the baked piecrust and refrigerate for at least 4 hours.

continued ⟶

Mousse

½ cup whole milk

1½ cups heavy cream

1 tablespoon matcha powder

1 tablespoon sugar

1 tablespoon agar agar powder

8 ounces white chocolate, coarsely chopped

Caramel

¼ cup water

¾ cup sugar

¾ cup heavy cream

2 tablespoons salted butter

My Favorite Whipped Cream (page 45)

½ recipe Moe's Piecrust (page 19)

5. To make the caramel: In a medium saucepan, combine the water with the sugar. Over medium-high heat, bring to a boil and watch it closely as the sugar begins to caramelize, darkening in color. When it reaches a nice, dark amber color, 5 to 6 minutes, remove from the heat and pour in the cream. You'll want to get your hand out of the way quickly to avoid the inevitable splatters. Once the sputtering has died down, stir until smooth and add the butter, stirring until it melts in completely. Set aside to cool, at least 1 hour.

6. Before serving, coat the top of the pie with My Favorite Whipped Cream, leaving a 2-inch border of green matcha filling around the edge of the crust. Pour the caramel sauce over the cream—a grid pattern looks very nice—and serve.

THAI TEA PIE

You'll notice that the tea-mousse pies all share one unexpected ingredient: white chocolate. Delicious as it can be, it's not included for its flavor. In fact, none of these pies particularly taste of white chocolate. Rather, the white chocolate gives the mousse texture and volume. You can imagine a pie like this one made with a cornstarch-thickened pudding, which would be creamy and wonderful in its own right. Or even a custard pie version. But because it (and the other tea pies) is made with a mousse filling, it has both a richness and airiness that really set it apart. And thanks to the strong flavor of the tea, the flavor of the white chocolate recedes into the background.

1. To make the crust: In a food processor, pulverize the puffed rice and corn flakes into a coarse meal. You don't want any big, discernible chunks of cereal, and you don't want it to be so fine that it resembles flour. Alternatively, you can put the cereal in a ziplock bag, push as much of the air out as possible, and run a rolling pin back and forth over the bag until the cereal is crushed.

2. In a large mixing bowl, combine the cereal crumbs, salt, flour, and butter. Use your hands to combine the butter with the dry ingredients by squeezing and smooshing the softened butter into the crumbs until the mixture comes together like a dough. You're done mixing when the mixture sticks together if you squeeze a pinch between your fingers.

3. Dump the dough into a 9-inch pie pan and use your fingertips to press it evenly over the bottom and up the sides of the pan. You want to make sure the thickness of the crust is uniform, particularly where the bottom meets the side.

4. Freeze for 2 hours while you prepare the filling.

5. To make the filling: In a small saucepan, combine the milk, ¼ cup of the cream, and the tea mix, and heat over medium heat until the cream begins to bubble and steam. Remove from the heat and steep the tea in the cream for 30 minutes. Strain through a fine-mesh sieve to remove any of the powder that didn't dissolve and return the infused cream mixture to the saucepan.

continued →

Crust

⅓ cup puffed rice cereal

⅓ cup corn flakes

¼ teaspoon kosher salt

⅓ cup all-purpose flour

½ cup salted butter, at room temperature

Filling

¼ cup whole milk

1¼ cups heavy cream

1 tablespoon plus 1 teaspoon Thai tea mix (I like Pantai Norasingh)

1 tablespoon sugar

⅛ teaspoon kosher salt

1 tablespoon agar agar powder

10 ounces white chocolate, coarsely chopped

6. Add the sugar, salt, and agar agar to the saucepan, and bring to a boil over medium heat, stirring constantly. Cook for 5 minutes, or until the mixture is thick and no longer grainy. Remove from the heat and transfer to a large heatproof bowl.

7. Add the white chocolate to the thickened Thai tea mixture, cover with plastic wrap, and let sit for 10 minutes, allowing the tea mixture to melt the white chocolate. Meanwhile, in a medium bowl, use an electric mixer to whip the remaining 1 cup cream until it holds soft peaks. Uncover the white chocolate and tea mixture and stir until the white chocolate is completely melted and the mixture is smooth and glossy. Fold in the whipped cream, one-third at a time. Be careful not to overwork the mousse: if you stir it too vigorously or too much, it will lose its volume.

8. Scoop the filling into the piecrust and refrigerate until completely chilled, at least 4 hours. Serve cold.

PEPPERMINT CHIP MOUSSE PIE WITH PEPPERMINT BARK

There are many pies that can do double duty during the holidays. Moe's Pumpkin Pie (page 180), Sweet Potato Pie (page 173), and Pecan Pie (page 202) often show up on both Thanksgiving and Christmas. This is not one of those pies. At the Pie Hole, we roll this one out in mid-December because it is 100 percent a Christmas pie. The peppermint-chip mousse is lovely in its own right, but the little shards of peppermint bark that garnish the pie are what really send it over the top. You'll need only a few pieces of bark for the pie. The rest is for munching.

1. Preheat the oven to 300°F.

2. To make the chocolate crust: In a food processor, pulverize the sandwich cookies, cream filling and all. You should have about 1½ cups. Add the butter, and pulse a few times to combine. You'll know the "dough" is done when it starts to clump together.

3. Dump the cookie mixture into a 9-inch pie pan and use your fingertips to press it evenly over the bottom and up the sides of the pan. You want to make sure the thickness of the crust is uniform, particularly where the bottom meets the side. Bake for 10 minutes, and then immediately reshape the crust using the back of a metal spoon. Set aside.

4. To make the mousse: In a medium saucepan, combine ¾ cup of the cream, the sugar, peppermint extract, and agar agar, and bring to a boil over medium heat, stirring constantly. Cook for 5 minutes, or until the mixture is thick and no longer grainy. Remove from the heat and transfer to a large heatproof bowl.

Chocolate Crust

20 cream-filled chocolate sandwich cookies (such as Oreos)

6 tablespoons salted butter, melted

Mousse

1½ cups heavy cream

¼ cup sugar

1½ teaspoons peppermint extract

2 teaspoons agar agar powder

9 ounces white chocolate, coarsely chopped

¾ cup semisweet chocolate chips

Peppermint Bark (page 150) for garnish

continued ⟶

5. Add the white chocolate and semisweet chocolate chips to the cream mixture, cover with plastic wrap, and let sit for 10 minutes to allow the cream to melt the chocolate. Meanwhile, in a large bowl, use an electric mixer to whip the remaining ¾ cup cream until soft peaks form. Uncover the white chocolate mixture and stir until the white chocolate is completely melted and the mixture is smooth and glossy. Fold in the whipped cream, one-third at a time. Be careful not to overwork the mousse: if you stir it too vigorously or too much, it will lose its volume.

6. Scoop the mousse into the pie shell. Use your hands to break up a few pieces of the peppermint bark and garnish the top with shards. Refrigerate completely, at least 4 hours. Serve cold.

 continued ⟶

ABOUT
16 OUNCES

PEPPERMINT BARK

**8 ounces semisweet
chocolate, chopped into
½-inch pieces**

2 tablespoons salted butter

**1 teaspoon peppermint
extract**

**8 ounces white chocolate,
chopped into ½-inch
pieces**

**6 peppermint candies or
2 candy canes, crushed**

1. Line a cookie sheet with aluminum foil, shiny-side up.

2. In the top of a double boiler or a heatproof bowl nestled in the top of a saucepan, with simmering water below, combine the semisweet chocolate and 1 tablespoon of the butter. Stir until the chocolate is completely melted. Remove from the heat and stir in ½ teaspoon of the peppermint extract.

3. Pour the melted chocolate onto the prepared cookie sheet, and use a spatula to spread it out in an even layer.

4. Clean and thoroughly dry the top of the double boiler (or bowl), place it over simmering water, and melt the white chocolate and the remaining 1 tablespoon butter. Stir until completely melted. Remove from the heat and stir in the remaining ½ teaspoon peppermint extract.

5. Pour the melted white chocolate over the semisweet chocolate layer and use a spatula to spread it out in an even layer. Scatter the crushed peppermints over the white chocolate. Set aside to cool completely, at least 2 hours.

BAILEYS MINT CHOCOLATE CREAM PIE

MAKES ONE 9-INCH PIE

This is like a chocolate after-dinner mint in pie form: a rich, chocolaty crust made with crushed Oreos and a creamy filling liberally dosed with Irish cream liqueur. And just as that cut-crystal bowl of after-dinner mints at the maître d's stand used to signal "fancy" at a restaurant, this pie feels a little luxe to me. With the bit of booze in the filling, it's the ideal pie for a wintertime holiday party.

1. Preheat the oven to 300°F.

2. To make the chocolate crust: In a food processor, pulverize the sandwich cookies, cream filling and all. You should have about 1½ cups. Add the butter, and pulse a few times to combine. You'll know the "dough" is done when it starts to clump together.

3. Put the cookie mixture in a 9-inch springform pan and use your fingertips to press it evenly over the bottom and up the sides of the pan. You want to make sure the thickness of the crust is uniform, particularly where the bottom meets the side. Bake for 10 minutes, and then immediately reshape the crust using the back of a metal spoon. Set aside to cool on a wire rack for at least 30 minutes.

4. To make the filling: In a large bowl, with an electric mixer at medium speed, combine the egg yolks and granulated sugar and beat until foamy. Add the cocoa powder, cornstarch, instant coffee, and salt, and continue beating until incorporated. Add the heavy cream, milk, and Irish cream liqueur, and beat until completely smooth. Transfer the mixture to a large saucepan and cook over medium heat, whisking constantly, until the filling begins to boil. Cook, stirring, until the mixture has thickened significantly, about 2 minutes. Remove from the heat and whisk in the butter and vanilla. Continue whisking until the butter melts completely and the mixture becomes nice and glossy. Set aside to cool, about 30 minutes.

Chocolate Crust

20 cream-filled chocolate sandwich cookies (I like Oreos)

6 tablespoons salted butter, melted

Filling

4 egg yolks

1½ cups granulated sugar

⅓ cup unsweetened cocoa powder

¼ cup cornstarch

½ teaspoon instant coffee crystals

Pinch of kosher salt

2½ cups heavy cream

½ cup whole milk

¼ cup Irish cream liqueur (such as Baileys)

1 tablespoon salted butter

1 tablespoon vanilla extract

continued →

continued →

Mint Whipped Cream

1 cup heavy cream

½ cup confectioners' sugar

1 tablespoon cornstarch

¼ teaspoon mint extract

3 drops green food coloring

Fresh mint leaves for garnish

Chocolate curls for garnish (optional; see sidebar)

5. Pour the filling into the chilled crust and smooth it out into a thick, even layer. Refrigerate the pie for 1 hour.

6. While the pie chills, make the mint whipped cream: In a large bowl, with an electric mixer, beat the cream until soft peaks begin to develop. With a spatula, stir in the confectioners' sugar, cornstarch, mint extract, and food coloring. Beat again until stiff peaks form.

7. Spread the whipped cream over the chocolate filling, leaving a 1-inch border along the edge of the crust, so the filling peeks through. Refrigerate until ready to serve. To serve, remove the sides of the springform pan, garnish with a few mint leaves, and scatter the chocolate curls over the top.

This probably isn't the way a pastry chef would do it, but I always make my chocolate curls with a milk chocolate bar and a vegetable peeler. I run the peeler along a short end of the bar and cut off a little sliver of chocolate, which curls very nicely. After peeling off a few curls, I flip to the opposite side of the bar, because my hand gets the chocolate too warm and the curls stop curling. Keep "peeler-ing" and flipping the bar until you have enough. I am always very generous when sprinkling curls over my desserts. The more you have, the nicer they look.

PEACHES AND CREAM PIE

In the very early days of the Pie Hole, there was no team of chefs digging through my recipe files or pulling their own creations out of what has sometimes seemed like thin air. The work of coming up with new pies to fill out our menu was left largely to me. Being an old-school baker, I took my inspiration from classic recipes, like this riff on my Blueberry Cream Pie (page 117) that swaps in ripe peaches for the blueberries. You cannot go wrong with peaches and cream. The sour cream gives the filling a touch of tartness, which goes really well with the bright, sweet flavor of the peaches.

½ recipe Moe's Piecrust (page 19)

1 pound fresh peaches

1 egg

1 cup sour cream

¾ cup sugar

2 tablespoons all-purpose flour

¼ teaspoon kosher salt

1. Roll out the crust, and lay it in a 9-inch pie pan. Trim and flute the edge according to the instructions on page 23. Set aside.

2. Preheat the oven to 400°F.

3. Fill a large pot halfway with water and bring it to a boil. While the water heats up, set up an ice bath: fill a large mixing bowl with water and an ample amount of ice cubes. With the sharp point of a paring knife, cut an X in the bottom of each peach. Put the peaches in the boiling water for about 1 minute, or until the skins begin to peel back from the cut. Remove the fruit with a slotted spoon and immediately transfer to the ice bath. Once the peaches are cool enough to handle, slip off the skins. Pit the peaches and slice ¼ inch thick.

4. In a medium bowl, whisk together the egg, sour cream, sugar, flour, and salt until well combined. Set aside about 10 peach slices, and gently fold the rest into the egg and sour cream mixture.

5. Dump the filling into the piecrust, and lay the reserved peach slices across the top of the filling. Bake for 25 minutes, or until the peaches on the top are nicely browned, and the filling is set.

6. Cool on a wire rack for 2 hours, and then refrigerate for at least 2 hours longer. Serve cold.

CEREAL KILLER PIE

This is a recipe you can really play with to fit your particular childhood memories by swapping out the Fruity Pebbles for another sugary cereal. Rainbow colored cereals look particularly good—but you can use Cocoa Puffs, Count Chocula, Frosted Flakes . . . anything, really. Though maybe not Grape-Nuts.

Vanilla Wafer Crust

36 vanilla wafers (I like Nilla Wafers)

6 tablespoons salted butter, melted

Filling

6 ounces cream cheese, at room temperature

3 tablespoons sugar

1 teaspoon vanilla extract

1 tablespoon maple syrup

1 tablespoon freshly squeezed lemon juice

½ cup heavy cream

1½ cups Fruity Pebbles or another sweet dry cereal (preferably a colorful one)

1. To make the vanilla wafer crust: In a food processor, pulverize the vanilla wafers, pulsing until the cookies are broken down into small, uniform crumbs. In a large mixing bowl, combine the wafer crumbs and butter, and stir until the mixture starts to come together like a dough. Press into an even layer in the bottom of a 9-inch pie pan. Refrigerate for at least 30 minutes.

2. To make the filling: In a large mixing bowl, use an electric mixer on medium speed to beat the cream cheese until smooth. Add the sugar and continue beating until thoroughly blended. Add the vanilla, maple syrup, and lemon juice and beat until incorporated. Pour in the cream and beat until the liquid is incorporated. Increase the mixer speed to medium-high and beat the cream cheese mixture until stiff peaks form. Fold in 1¼ cups of the Fruity Pebbles.

3. Scoop the cream cheese filling into the chilled vanilla wafer crust. Refrigerate for at least 4 hours. Just before serving, scatter the remaining ¼ cup cereal over the top. Serve cold.

VEGAN COCONUT CREAM PIE

MAKES ONE 9-INCH PIE

There's a lot of milk, butter, and eggs involved in making a cream pie. But that doesn't mean a vegan version can't be just as good. In fact, the best vegan baking should feel like you're gaining something from the recipe rather than trying to mimic a dairy version. This coconut cream pie, which even has a crust made of coconut flakes and coconut oil, is a prime example: the crust is an ideal foil for the smooth cornstarch pudding filling, shot through with coconut flakes. There's no milk, butter, or eggs, and you won't even miss them. Add a sprinkle of toasted coconut flakes for garnish if you'd like.

1. Preheat the oven to 325°F.

2. To make the crust: In a medium bowl, toss together the coconut flakes and coconut oil. Press the mixture into the bottom and up the sides of a 9-inch pie pan. You want to make sure the thickness of the crust is uniform, particularly where the bottom meets the side. Bake for about 20 minutes, until the crust is brown. Begin checking it after 15 minutes to make sure it doesn't get too brown or burn. The sides of the crust will slip down the pan during baking, so use the back of a metal spoon to immediately press the crust back into place. Set aside to cool.

3. To make the filling: In a medium saucepan, combine the coconut milk and vegan butter. Heat over medium heat until the butter melts into the milk. Add the sugar, cornstarch, and salt. Bring to a boil, stirring constantly. Make sure that any clumps of cornstarch are broken up and nothing is sticking to the bottom of the pan. Boil for 3 minutes, stirring constantly, until the pudding is very thick and will hold its shape when scooped up in a spoon. Remove from the heat and whisk in the coconut flakes and vanilla.

4. Pour the coconut pudding into the baked pie shell. Press plastic wrap onto the top of the filling and cool on a wire rack for 2 hours. Then refrigerate for at least 2 hours longer. Serve cold.

Crust

1⅓ cups unsweetened coconut flakes

2 tablespoons coconut oil, melted if solid

Filling

4 cups full-fat coconut milk

2 tablespoons vegan butter (I like Country Crock plant butter)

1 cup sugar

¼ cup cornstarch

Pinch of kosher salt

1 cup unsweetened coconut flakes

2 teaspoons vanilla extract

CHAPTER 5

custard pies

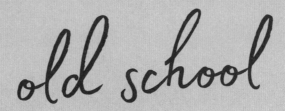

old school

Like cream pies, custard pies are a thrifty dessert. Made with little more than milk, butter, eggs, and some kind of flavoring, they're cheap to shop for—especially if, like Moe, you have an endless supply of eggs.

The chicken coop at Moe's is long gone, so I have to buy my eggs now. But for me there's still a certain nostalgic charm to a custard pie. While I am in Los Angeles on occasion, I spend most of my time in Pennsylvania, and I have an elderly neighbor in Berwick, Hank, whom I sometimes bake pies for. Plain custard is his favorite: just eggs, milk, and sugar, flavored with a little bit of vanilla and some nutmeg. He knows that I make pie (my reputation as the Pie Lady sometimes precedes me, even in pie country), and when we first met, he very slyly told me that he liked plain custard pie—not coconut custard, which is his wife's favorite.

Hank's getting on in years, and it's not easy for him to come across the street to visit, but he always makes a point to do so. On occasion, I make the effort in return, cracking egg after egg after egg and whipping them up with sugar and milk to make him a custard pie. When a pie is as simple as this one, the little touches really get a chance to stand out. You could, perhaps, call mine a nutmeg custard pie, because a little pinch of the spice stands out so wonderfully against the rich sweetness of the eggy filling. If a bit of spice and vanilla can shine in what amounts to a plain pie, what else is worth trying? Like a cream pie filling, a custard filling is a blank canvas. You can flavor it with apples or rhubarb, maple syrup, or sweet corn. Or it can just taste like a plain old custard pie, because sometimes that's the most comforting flavor of all.

Most baking cookbooks recommend the same doneness test for cakes and muffins: Insert a cake tester, the point of a knife, or a toothpick in the middle. If it comes out clean, it's done. The same test holds true for pies, but the location does not: For custard pies and others with a thick, baked filling, you want to check midway between the edge of the crust and the center of the pie. Why? Your filling will continue to set as it cools. That's why you test in a different place, and why you want the filling to still be slightly jiggly when you pull a pie from the oven. If you're pulling it out when the center is already firm, then you're going to end up with a pie that's overbaked.

MOE'S CUSTARD PIE

2½ cups whole milk

4 eggs

½ cup sugar

¼ teaspoon kosher salt

½ teaspoon vanilla extract

½ recipe Moe's Piecrust
(page 19)

Freshly grated nutmeg
for garnish

This is my grandmother's plain custard pie, which is what I make for my neighbor Hank. Don't be fooled by the simple ingredients; the whole is more than the sum of the parts here. Rather than a plain custard pie, think of it as a minimalist one. This basic recipe is the basis for many other pies, both old school and new school, found throughout this chapter. Really, you could use this filling base, flavor it with just about anything—infuse the milk, change the sweetener, pour it over chopped fruit—and you'd probably have a delicious pie. But for starters, try this more classic approach. I think you'll understand what Hank sees in it.

1. Preheat the oven to 350°F.

2. In a small saucepan, heat the milk over low heat until tiny bubbles begin to form around the edge and the milk begins to steam. Remove the scalded milk from the heat.

3. In a large bowl, whisk together the eggs, sugar, salt, and vanilla. Gradually whisk in the scalded milk.

4. Roll out the crust, and lay it in a 9-inch pie pan. Trim and flute the edge according to the instructions on page 23. Pour the filling into the crust, and sprinkle the top with nutmeg.

5. Bake for 35 to 40 minutes, or until a knife inserted halfway between the center of the pie and the edge comes out clean. Cool on a wire rack for 2 hours, and then refrigerate until completely chilled, 2 to 3 hours. Serve cold.

COCONUT CUSTARD PIE

When I was growing up, this was always a special-occasion kind of pie, and it really shows how versatile custard pies can be. There's only one extra ingredient, ½ cup of coconut flakes sprinkled over the custard, but it changes the pie completely. If a plain custard pie (see opposite) was for Easter brunch, this pie is what we ate for dessert at a formal Sunday dinner, the kind of meal that we would have in the dining room instead of at the kitchen table, on the good china. It's just as fitting for birthdays or other celebrations that have a touch of class.

2½ cups whole milk

4 eggs

½ cup sugar

¼ teaspoon kosher salt

½ teaspoon vanilla extract

½ recipe Moe's Piecrust (page 19)

½ cup sweetened coconut flakes

1. Preheat the oven to 350°F.

2. In a small saucepan, heat the milk over low heat until tiny bubbles begin to form around the edge and the milk begins to steam. Remove the scalded milk from the heat.

3. In a large bowl, whisk together the eggs, sugar, salt, and vanilla. Gradually whisk in the scalded milk.

4. Roll out the crust, and lay it in a 9-inch pie pan. Trim and flute the edge according to the instructions on page 23. Pour the filling into the crust, and scatter the coconut flakes over the top.

5. Bake for 35 to 40 minutes, or until a knife inserted halfway between the center of the pie and the edge comes out clean. Cool on a wire rack for 2 hours, and then move to the refrigerator and chill for 2 more hours. Serve cold.

APPLE CUSTARD PIE

Apple custard was always for holidays, a fall kind of thing. When I didn't have enough apples to make an apple pie, I'd make this one instead. And really that's preferable to me: rich, creamy pies tend to be my favorite, not fruit pies. With this recipe I can scratch the apple pie itch for family and guests while I still get to enjoy the kind of eggy custard filling that I love most.

½ recipe Moe's Piecrust
(page 19)

6 to 8 tart apples, such as
McIntosh, peeled, cored,
and sliced (about 3 cups)

¾ cup sugar

3 tablespoons all-purpose
flour

½ teaspoon kosher salt

¼ cup heavy cream

1 egg

Ground cinnamon

Cheddar cheese for serving
(optional)

1. Preheat the oven to 375°F.

2. Roll out the crust, and lay it in a 9-inch pie pan. Trim and flute the edge according to the instructions on page 23. Arrange the apple slices in the bottom of the pie shell—be as artful or as messy as you'd like.

3. In a medium bowl, stir together the sugar, flour, and salt. Add the cream and egg, and whisk until thoroughly combined. Pour the custard over the apples, and sprinkle the top with cinnamon.

4. Cover loosely with aluminum foil and bake for 1 hour. Remove the foil, and bake for 15 minutes more, or until a knife inserted halfway between the center of the pie and the edge comes out clean and the apples are tender.

5. Serve warm with Cheddar cheese, if desired, or refrigerate until completely chilled, 2 to 3 hours, and serve cold.

MILK PIE

This is a true relic from the Depression, when ingredients and money were scarce, but good pie was always around. On the recipe card from my Grammy (not Moe, my other grandmother) it says to "mix the ingredients together with your fingers," and she really did make this pie with just her hands. She would use her fingers to mix the flour and sugar, put the dry ingredients in the crust, and add the milk, stirring again with a finger and then popping the pie in the oven. The pie takes a long time to bake, but that's how the simplest of ingredients become something delicious.

½ recipe Moe's Piecrust
(page 19)

1 cup sugar

2 heaping tablespoons
all-purpose flour

Whole milk for filling
the piecrust

2 tablespoons salted
butter, cut into pieces

Ground cinnamon

1. Preheat the oven to 350°F.

2. Roll out the crust, and lay it in a 9-inch pie pan. Trim and flute the edge according to the instructions on page 23. Set aside.

3. In a small bowl, mix together the sugar and flour, with your fingertips if you would like to, just like Grammy. Dump the sugar mixture into the bottom of the piecrust, and then fill with milk to just ¼ inch below the top of the crust. Stir gently—you can use your index finger—until the sugar mixture is blended into the milk. Add the chunks of butter, and sprinkle with lots of cinnamon.

4. Bake for 1 hour and 15 minutes, or until the filling is slightly jiggly in the middle but not soupy. Cool on a wire rack for 2 hours, and then refrigerate until completely chilled, about 2 hours more. Serve cold.

BUTTERMILK PIE

½ recipe Moe's Piecrust
(page 19)

4 eggs

1½ cups sugar

6 tablespoons salted
butter, melted

2 tablespoons all-purpose
flour

1 teaspoon vanilla extract

½ teaspoon kosher salt

¾ cup buttermilk

⅓ cup chopped walnuts

This is very much a Southern pie, and as such was not part of my early childhood in Pennsylvania. I'm not sure who introduced it to our family (maybe Aunt Em, the wife of my dad's uncle, who lived in Baltimore), but there was a before and after moment: for many years there was no buttermilk pie, and then it showed up, and we made it quite a lot.

One thing that sets this recipe apart from other buttermilk pies are the walnuts, which sit on top of the filling, adding a little texture and richness.

1. Preheat the oven to 350°F.

2. Roll out the crust, and lay it in a 9-inch pie pan. Trim and flute the edge according to the instructions on page 23. Set aside.

3. In a large bowl, with an electric mixer on medium-high speed, beat the eggs. Add the sugar, butter, flour, vanilla, and salt, and continue to beat until well blended. Turn down the mixer speed to low, and slowly add the buttermilk, beating until thoroughly combined. Pour the filling into the pie shell, and scatter the walnuts on top.

4. Bake for 40 to 45 minutes, or until a knife inserted halfway between the center of the pie and the edge comes out clean and the top is golden. Cool on a wire rack for 2 hours and then refrigerate until completely chilled, 2 to 3 hours. Serve cold.

SWEET POTATO PIE

During the holidays, we always have Moe's Pumpkin Pie (page 180) and sweet potato pie—and often Pecan Pie (page 202); Pear, Cranberry, and Ginger Pie (page 50); and maybe a Peanut Butter Crunch Pie (page 95), too. It's a lot of pies. The pumpkin and sweet potato pies are easily confused, and after years of "Mom! Which one is the pumpkin pie?," I decided to solve the problem. Because I had pecans around, I started pressing a few into the top of this pie to mark it. It's a nice decorative touch, too, but the pie looks fine on its own.

1. Preheat the oven to 400°F.

2. In a large bowl, combine the sweet potatoes, brown sugar, salt, cinnamon, and nutmeg.

3. In a medium bowl, whisk the eggs together and then whisk in the sour cream, milk, and butter. Add this liquid mixture to the sweet potatoes and stir to combine well.

4. Roll out the crust, and lay it in a 9-inch pie pan. Trim and flute the edge according to the instructions on page 23.

5. Dump the sweet potato filling into the pie shell. If you like, place the pecans in a circle around the edge of the pie.

6. Bake for 45 minutes, or until the top is lightly browned and the tip of a knife inserted halfway between the center of the pie and the edge comes out clean. I like this pie cold. Cool on a wire rack for 2 hours, and then refrigerate until chilled, at least 2 hours, and serve.

1¼ cups mashed sweet potatoes (see sidebar)

½ cup packed dark brown sugar

½ teaspoon kosher salt

¼ teaspoon ground cinnamon

Pinch of freshly grated nutmeg

2 eggs

½ cup sour cream

¼ cup whole milk

1 tablespoon salted butter, melted

½ recipe Moe's Piecrust (page 19)

12 pecan halves for garnish (optional)

Whether my sweet potatoes are purple or orange, I like to boil them for pies rather than bake them. To boil them, wash and peel them, and then cut them into 1-inch chunks. Put them in a large saucepan, cover with cold water, and bring to a boil over medium heat. Lower the heat and simmer, uncovered, until the sweet potatoes are very tender, 15 to 20 minutes. Drain and cool, and then you're ready to make pie!

KEY LIME PIE

There are two major lessons I've learned in a lifetime of making different iterations of this pie. The first is that while you *can* start with milk, cream, and sugar instead of cracking open a can of sweetened condensed milk, the extra time and effort don't really pay off. The second lesson has to do with the only other variable in this recipe, and that's the limes. I've made plenty of lime pies in my life—and for the longest time, there probably weren't enough fresh Key limes in all of Pennsylvania to make a single pie. But there's a reason that Key lime pie is what people know and love. The little limes have a special, deep citrus flavor to them, and it's really worth putting in the extra effort to get, and squeeze, the right kind of lime.

Graham Cracker Piecrust (page 29)

5 egg yolks

One 14-ounce can sweetened condensed milk (such as Eagle Brand)

½ cup freshly squeezed Key lime juice (10 or 12 Key limes)

My Favorite Whipped Cream (optional; page 45)

Grated lime zest for garnish (optional)

1. Bake the graham cracker crust. Set aside. Keep the oven at 350°F.

2. In a large bowl, whisk together the egg yolks. Continue whisking while you pour in the sweetened condensed milk in a slow, steady stream. Whisk until well blended, and then whisk in the lime juice. Pour the filling into the graham cracker crust.

3. Bake for 12 to 15 minutes, or until the filling is almost set but still slightly moist and jiggly in the middle. Cool on a wire rack to room temperature, at least 2 hours, and refrigerate for at least 2 hours. If you like, before serving, spread the whipped cream on top and dust with lime zest.

MOM'S LEMON CUSTARD PIE

½ recipe Moe's Piecrust
(page 19)

1 cup sugar

1 tablespoon salted butter,
at room temperature

3 tablespoons all-purpose
flour

⅛ teaspoon kosher salt

2 eggs, separated

1 cup whole milk

Grated zest of 1 lemon

¼ cup freshly squeezed
lemon juice

My Favorite Whipped
Cream (optional; page 45)
for serving

Like Dot's Lemon Sponge Pie (page 60), this is a brightly flavored citrus pie that is both easy to make and very impressive. When my mom was a young housewife trying to impress, there weren't always a lot of options for fresh ingredients during the winter. But she could count on finding lemons at the grocery store, and she must have been grateful that so many pies were flavored with them. This was her favorite of the lot, and she'd often make it for Sunday dinner. This pie always brings back memories of watching my parents play a card game called "horse and pepper" out on the picnic table on the backyard patio, while everyone enjoyed a slice of lemon custard pie.

1. Preheat the oven to 325°F.

2. Roll out the dough, and lay it in a 9-inch pie pan. Trim and flute the edge according to the instructions on page 23. Set aside.

3. In a large bowl, with an electric mixer at medium speed, cream the sugar and butter until light and fluffy, about 5 minutes. Beat in the flour, salt, egg yolks, and milk, and continue beating until well blended. Add the lemon zest and juice and beat until completely incorporated.

4. In a medium bowl, with clean beaters, use the electric mixer to beat the egg whites at medium-high speed until stiff peaks form. Gently fold the egg whites into the lemon mixture, and spoon the filling into the pie shell.

5. Bake for 1 hour, or until a knife inserted halfway between the center of the pie and the edge comes out clean and the top is lightly browned. Cool completely on the counter, at least 4 hours. Top with whipped cream, if desired, and serve.

SHOOFLY PIE

MAKES ONE
9-INCH PIE

This Pennsylvania Dutch recipe is probably the most distinctly Pennsylvanian pie of all. It is thought to have originally been made as a sponge cake, hence the quick-leavened filling, which gets its airiness from the baking soda. At some point, someone baked the cake inside of a piecrust, and no one looked back. It's now a pie recipe, through and through. "Shoofly" is probably a reference to what happens when you cool a pie filled with a sticky, molasses-rich filling on an open windowsill: the flies show up. So part of the work of baking a shoofly pie was actually shooing flies away after pulling it out of the oven. However, I can attest to the fact that the pie is just as gooey and delicious if you don't have to chase off any insects.

1 cup all-purpose flour

¾ cup packed dark brown sugar

2 tablespoons vegetable shortening

1 egg

1 cup mild-flavored molasses (not blackstrap)

1 cup hot water

1 teaspoon baking soda

½ recipe Moe's Piecrust (page 19)

1. Preheat the oven to 375°F.

2. In a large bowl, stir together the flour and brown sugar, and use a pastry blender or your fingers to work in the shortening. Set aside 1 cup of the mixture for a crumb topping, and leave the rest in the bowl.

3. In a medium bowl, stir together the egg, molasses, and ¾ cup of the hot water. In a small dish, dissolve the baking soda in the remaining ¼ cup hot water. Add the baking soda and water to the molasses mixture, stirring to combine. Dump the molasses mixture into the flour mixture in the bowl, and stir together to combine. Set the filling aside.

4. Roll out the crust, and lay it in a 9-inch pie pan. Trim and flute the edge according to the instructions on page 23. Spread out the filling in the pie shell, and scatter the reserved 1 cup of the flour and brown sugar mixture over the top.

5. Bake for 10 minutes, then lower the heat to 350°F and bake for 30 minutes more, or until the top is brown and a knife inserted halfway between the center of the pie and the edge comes out clean. This has a more cakey filling than the other pies in this chapter, so it will not be jiggly. Cool on a wire rack for 2 hours (taking care to shoo away any flies), and then refrigerate for at least 2 hours longer. Serve cold.

MOE'S PUMPKIN PIE

1½ cups pumpkin puree, homemade (see sidebar, opposite) or canned

1 cup sugar

1 teaspoon kosher salt

1½ teaspoons freshly grated nutmeg

1½ cups whole milk

4 eggs

1½ teaspoons vanilla extract

½ recipe Moe's Piecrust (page 19)

Ground cinnamon

My Favorite Whipped Cream (optional; page 45) for serving

This is the pie that Moe was locally famous for in Berwick, Pennsylvania, my hometown. She used to bring it to various holiday events, especially around Thanksgiving. I, too, was a fan, and when I was eight or nine, I tried to re-create it in my mother's kitchen. Let's just say that I've gotten much better at baking this pie in the years since.

We've been serving this pie at the Pie Hole since the very beginning, and one customer from those early days was pretty insistent that I give him the recipe. He claimed it was the best pumpkin pie he ever ate (he was the first of many guests to say that). I refused, so he offered to pay me for it. "I'll give you $100,000!" he said. I still demurred, but here we are all these years later, and you have it for the price of a book, just as Moe made it.

1. Preheat the oven to 400°F.

2. In a large bowl, combine the pumpkin, sugar, salt, and nutmeg, and mash together with a wooden spoon until well combined. In a medium bowl, whisk together the milk, eggs, and vanilla. Pour the milk mixture into the pumpkin and stir to blend well.

3. Roll out the crust, and lay it in a 9-inch pie pan. Trim and flute the edge according to the instructions on page 23. Spread out the pumpkin filling in the pie shell, and sprinkle the top with cinnamon.

4. Bake for 30 to 40 minutes, or until a knife inserted halfway between the center of the pie and the edge comes out clean. Cool on the counter until room temperature, at least 2 hours, before serving. Or refrigerate until you're ready to eat. Serve with whipped cream, if desired.

Canned pumpkin works wonderfully for Moe's Pumpkin Pie, but I love to roast a whole pumpkin and puree the flesh myself. If you want to try it, you'll need a good baking variety: Look for a sugar pumpkin, which is also called a pie pumpkin or sweet pumpkin. Though they're not as flavorful, I'll still sometimes use decorative fall pumpkins for pies, too, just so they don't go to waste. The flavor of your puree will really be determined by what type of pumpkin you use, and that's the fun of making it from scratch. Winter squash work, too, so you can make a butternut squash pie or hubbard squash pie, or whatever variety you want to try.

Split the pumpkin in half and scoop out the seeds and stringy pulp that surrounds them. Preheat the oven to 375°F. Place the gutted pumpkin halves, cut-side down, in a 9 by 13-inch baking dish, and add about ½ inch of water. Cover with aluminum foil and bake for about 45 minutes, or until a paring knife stuck into the rind pushes through easily. Let the pumpkin cool completely, at least 1 hour, and then with an ice cream scoop, remove the tender flesh from the skins. Transfer to a blender, 2 cups at a time, and puree until smooth. Your homemade pumpkin puree is ready to use. The puree can be stored in a sealed container in the fridge.

Moe's original recipe provided ingredients and directions for making one pie and for making two. But she didn't simply double each ingredient for two pies. Some ingredients listed for two pies were one and half times the amount for one pie. For reasons that are beyond me, it just works, and I still follow the double-pie recipe religiously. When I was a child, I used to marvel at how smart Moe was to figure this all out, and have two pies with an equal amount of pumpkin filling in each one. Actually, I still do. To make two pies, you'll need 2 cups pumpkin puree, 1½ cups sugar, 1½ teaspoons kosher salt, 2 teaspoons freshly grated nutmeg, 2 teaspoons vanilla extract, 2 cups whole milk, 6 eggs, a full recipe of Moe's Piecrust (page 19), and ground cinnamon.

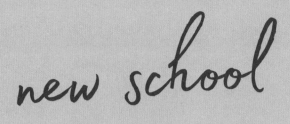

new school

When I was growing up, a pie in a new flavor was rare. Sometimes we'd come by a new recipe, shared by a friend or cut out of a magazine. But more often than not, "new" recipes were more of the same. My mom might bake the Apricot-Nectarine Pie (page 52), which tasted new and exciting. But it was really just a slightly different version of a peach pie. "New" was a relative term. So when I described the "new-new" recipes as we were developing recipes before we opened the first Pie Hole in the L.A. Arts District, I got a lot of weird looks from friends and family. Pies made with grapefruit? And sweet corn? But when my mom became a Maple Custard Pie (page 194) convert, I knew I could win over anyone once they actually tried a bite of my brand-new pies.

When I first told my mom that I had reworked Moe's Custard Pie (page 164) recipe to feature a glug of maple syrup, she was wary, to say the least. She didn't understand why I'd want to do that. But it soon became her favorite pie. She's made a lot of custard pies throughout her life, often plain custard, and sometimes Coconut Custard Pie (page 165) for a special occasion. But now all she wants to make is maple custard pie.

SALTED HONEY CUSTARD PIE

½ recipe Moe's Piecrust
(page 19)

5 egg yolks

1¼ cups heavy cream

½ cup honey

⅓ cup sugar

½ teaspoon kosher salt,
or to taste

This is basically Moe's Custard Pie (page 164), with a little bit of honey and an extra pinch of salt stirred into the filling. But those small tweaks make a huge difference. This is a perennial favorite at the Pie Hole, and whenever we take it off the menu, requests for its return start pouring in. Luckily, it's a very easy pie to bake at home! Although any honey will do the trick for the filling, you can experiment with different types. If you like a particular monofloral honey—buckwheat? mesquite?—give it a shot. It's bound to be good.

1. Preheat the oven to 375°F.

2. Roll out the crust, and lay it in a 9-inch pie pan. Use the tines of a fork to poke holes in the bottom and sides, which will keep the crust from bubbling. Trim and flute the edge according to the instructions on page 23. Bake for 15 to 20 minutes, or until the dough is set but not browned. Set aside to cool.

3. Lower the oven temperature to 350°F.

4. In a large bowl, whisk together the egg yolks. Whisk in the cream, honey, sugar, and salt, and continue whisking until smooth. Pour the mixture into the pie shell.

5. Bake for 20 minutes. Rotate the pie 180 degrees and bake for 10 to 15 minutes longer, or until the middle is nicely browned and a knife inserted halfway between the center of the pie and the edge comes out clean. The filling should be jiggly but not soupy. Cool on a wire rack for at least 2 hours, and then refrigerate for 2 hours more. Serve cold.

RHUBARB CUSTARD PIE

There's a patch of rhubarb in nearly every backyard in Northeast Pennsylvania, so it still makes me laugh that this grows-like-a-weed option for pie filling is rather hard to come by in Southern California. The fact that rhubarb is abundant and often free is surely part of the reason it was once called the "pie plant." But rhubarb pie recipes aren't all about thrift. Rhubarb happens to be incredibly delicious, and lends a wonderful tartness to pies that can't really be replicated by any other fruit filling. While Rhubarb Pie (page 43) is the classic, there are plenty of other rhubarb-based pies out there, including this recipe, in which the tart, ruby-red slices dot a rich custard filling.

½ recipe Moe's Piecrust (page 19)

1½ pounds rhubarb, red part of stem only, cut into ½-inch pieces (about 3 cups)

1 cup sugar

3 tablespoons all-purpose flour

½ teaspoon kosher salt

⅓ cup heavy cream

1 egg

1. Preheat the oven to 375°F.

2. Roll out the crust, and lay it in a 9-inch pie pan. Trim and flute the edge according to the instructions on page 23. Put the rhubarb in the crust.

3. In a medium bowl, stir together the sugar, flour, and salt. Whisk in the cream and egg until well blended. Pour over the rhubarb in the pie shell and cover loosely with aluminum foil.

4. Bake for 1 hour. Remove the foil and bake for another 10 to 15 minutes, or until the rhubarb is completely tender. Serve the pie warm, or cool until room temperature, about 2 hours. It's up to you!

CHOCOLATE BROWNIE CUSTARD PIE

MAKES ONE 9-INCH PIE

Aside from making a pie, one of the most comforting bits of home baking is mixing up a pan of brownies. This recipe, then, is the best of both worlds: it takes those brownies and transforms them into a whole pie. After it's baked, the filling recalls the rich, cakey texture of good brownies, which contrasts wonderfully with the flaky crust.

2½ tablespoons unsweetened cocoa powder

1 cup salted butter, melted

1¾ cups sugar

3 eggs

2 teaspoons vanilla extract

¼ teaspoon kosher salt

½ recipe Moe's Piecrust (page 19)

1. Preheat the oven to 300°F.

2. Put the cocoa powder in a large bowl. Slowly pour in the butter, whisking as you pour. Continue whisking until no clumps are left, about 2 minutes. Whisk in the sugar until completely incorporated. Add the eggs, vanilla, and salt, whisking to blend completely.

3. Roll out the crust, and lay it in a 9-inch pie pan. Trim and flute the edge according to the instructions on page 23. Pour the filling into the piecrust.

4. Bake for 45 to 50 minutes, or until firmly set—just like a brownie. This is a more cakey filling, so it won't be jiggly in the middle. Serve the pie warm, or cool until room temperature, up to 2 hours.

SWEET CORN CUSTARD PIE

This is a recipe that I developed before the first Pie Hole opened, during those high-summer weeks when the fresh sweet corn from the local farm stand tastes almost as sweet as a peach or strawberry. (California is rightfully famous for its produce, but nothing can hold a candle to Pennsylvania summer sweet corn.) Served at a family supper, this pie could stand in for a vegetable side dish. But if you do bring it out at the end of a meal, trust that any skepticism about eating vegetables for dessert will disappear after the first bite. Just remember that it needs to cool for a good 3 hours before serving, so make it well ahead of time.

½ recipe Moe's Piecrust (page 19)

3 ears fresh corn or 1½ cups thawed frozen corn or canned corn

1⅔ cups heavy cream

¾ cup sugar

1 teaspoon vanilla extract

Pinch of kosher salt

4 egg yolks

2 egg whites

1. Preheat the oven to 375°F. Roll out the crust, and lay it in a 9-inch pie pan. Use the tines of a fork to poke holes in the bottom and sides, which will keep the crust from bubbling. Trim and flute the edge according to the instructions on page 23. Bake for 35 to 40 minutes, or until golden brown. Set aside to cool completely. Lower the oven temperature to 350°F.

2. If using fresh sweet corn, husk the ears and microwave on medium, one at a time, for 4 minutes. Cut the cooked corn off the cob and measure out 1½ cups.

3. In a blender, combine ¾ cup of the corn, ⅔ cup of the cream, and all of the sugar. Pulse until the corn is chopped but not completely pureed, five to seven quick pulses.

4. In a large bowl, whisk together the remaining 1 cup cream, the vanilla, salt, and egg yolks until completely blended. Stir in the corn mixture and the remaining ¾ cup whole kernels.

5. In a medium bowl, use an electric mixer to whip the egg whites until soft peaks form, about 4 minutes. Gently fold the egg whites into the corn mixture until just combined, being careful not to fold too many times. Pour the filling into the partially baked pie shell.

6. Bake for 45 to 50 minutes, or until the top is dark golden brown and a knife inserted halfway between the center of the pie and the edge comes out clean.

7. Remove from the oven, cover with tented aluminum foil, and cool on a wire rack for at least 2 hours. Refrigerate until completely chilled, at least 2 hours. Serve cold.

GRAPEFRUIT PIE

½ recipe Moe's Piecrust
(page 19)

5 egg yolks

¾ cup plus 2 tablespoons
freshly squeezed grapefruit
juice (preferably pink)

One 14-ounce can
sweetened condensed milk

My Favorite Whipped
Cream (optional; page 45)
for serving

A lot of recipes in this cookbook call for lemons: They're juiced into fillings, and the fragrant zest perfumes a few piecrusts. Whole slices of lemon simmered in sugar syrup decorate the very beautiful Candied Lemon Chess Pie (page 69). But the rest of the wide, wide world of citrus? Save for an occasional orange and lime, it might as well not exist. When I first came to California, I was amazed at the variety of citrus fruit you could get, from the rosy skins of the blood oranges to the huge, pale Oro Blanco grapefruits. I thought there had to be a way to move beyond lemons and use some of this other wonderful citrus in pies. This pie was one of our earliest efforts at the Pie Hole, and it set us apart from other bakeries when we first opened in L.A.'s Arts District. Even in Southern California, no one had seen a tart, pink pie made with grapefruit before! You can use any variety of grapefruit, including those Oro Blancos, but I prefer the color you get from a pink or Ruby Red.

1. Preheat the oven to 375°F.

2. Roll out the crust, and lay it in a 9-inch pie pan. Use the tines of a fork to poke holes in the bottom and sides, which will keep the crust from bubbling. Trim and flute the edge according to the instructions on page 23. Bake for 35 to 40 minutes, or until golden brown. Set aside to cool completely. Lower the oven temperature to 350°F.

3. In a large bowl, use an electric mixer on medium speed to beat the egg yolks until they turn pale yellow and thicken slightly, about 5 minutes. While still beating, slowly add the grapefruit juice, and then the condensed milk, and continue beating until just combined. Pour the filling into the parbaked piecrust.

4. Bake for 15 minutes, or until the filling starts to set but is still a little loose and shaky in the middle, and the top is nicely browned. This bakes up quickly!

5. Cool on a wire rack for at least 2 hours, and then refrigerate for at least 2 hours. Serve cold, with whipped cream, if you like. But I prefer a pretty pink slice all on its own.

JAPANESE SWEET POTATO PIE

MAKES ONE 9-INCH PIE

Japanese sweet potatoes are gorgeous things; their flesh is a rich, deep purple color and they have a wonderful sweet, earthy flavor. You could, of course, use them to make a standard sweet potato pie, which just happens to be purple. But if you're going to turn this pie's color on its head, why not play around with the flavors, too? The filling for this pie is enriched with coconut milk and topped with toasty bits of coconut flakes and melting mini-marshmallows.

1. Preheat the oven to 375°F.

2. Roll out the crust, and lay it in a 9-inch pie pan. Use the tines of a fork to poke holes in the bottom and sides, which will keep the crust from bubbling. Trim and flute the edge according to the instructions on page 23. Bake for 15 to 20 minutes, or until the dough is set but not browned. Set aside to cool. Lower the oven temperature to 350°F.

3. In a large bowl, stir together the sweet potatoes, coconut milk, sugar, butter, eggs, vanilla, cinnamon, and salt, and continue stirring until well combined. Pour into the parbaked pie shell and bake for 40 to 45 minutes, or until the filling is set and a knife inserted halfway between the center of the pie and the edge comes out clean. The top will be browned a little, but you will still be able to tell the filling is purple!

4. Cool completely on the counter, at least 2 hours.

5. Toast the coconut flakes: In a small nonstick pan, heat the coconut flakes over low heat, stirring frequently, until they turn toasty brown, 5 to 7 minutes.

6. Arrange the mini-marshmallows over the top of the pie and caramelize with a kitchen torch. Alternatively, you can brown the marshmallows under the broiler. Place the oven rack at least 6 inches away from the heat. Broil on high for 3 minutes, or until golden brown, checking frequently. Garnish with the toasted coconut flakes and, if desired, a few dollops of whipped cream, and serve.

½ recipe Moe's Piecrust (page 19)

2 cups cooked and mashed Japanese sweet potatoes (about 1½ pounds sweet potatoes; see sidebar on page 173 for cooking instructions)

1 cup coconut milk

½ cup sugar

3 tablespoons salted butter, melted

3 eggs

1 teaspoon vanilla extract

½ teaspoon ground cinnamon

½ teaspoon kosher salt

¼ cup unsweetened coconut flakes

2 cups mini-marshmallows

My Favorite Whipped Cream (optional; page 45) for serving

MAPLE CUSTARD PIE

½ recipe Moe's Piecrust
(page 19)

1¼ cups heavy cream

½ cup pure maple syrup
(I prefer the one labeled
Grade A | Dark Color and
Robust Flavor)

⅓ cup sugar

½ teaspoon vanilla extract

4 egg yolks

Pinch of kosher salt

When my mom first heard the idea for this pie, she couldn't believe it. "Put maple syrup in a pie?" But she has gone from being incredulous to being this pie's biggest booster. When I make it at home—and I make it a lot, because now it's her favorite—she always asks everyone, "Have you tried this before? Have you ever heard of a maple custard pie before?"

The base is Moe's Custard Pie (page 164). But in addition to the eggs, sugar, and cream, there are a few glugs of maple syrup, which give the pie a wonderfully warm, sweet, breakfast-y flavor.

1. Preheat the oven to 375°F.

2. Roll out the crust, and lay it in a 9-inch pie pan. Use the tines of a fork to poke holes in the bottom and sides, which will keep the crust from bubbling. Trim and flute the edge according to the instructions on page 23. Bake for 15 to 20 minutes, or until the dough is set but not browned. Set aside to cool.

3. Lower the oven temperature to 350°F.

4. In a large bowl, whisk together the cream, maple syrup, sugar, vanilla, eggs, and salt, and continue whisking until smooth. Pour into the parbaked pie shell.

5. Bake for 20 minutes. Rotate the pie 180 degrees and bake for 10 to 15 minutes longer, until the middle is nicely browned. The filling should be jiggly, not soupy. Cool on a wire rack for at least 2 hours, and then refrigerate for at least 2 hours. Serve cold.

VEGAN LEMON CUSTARD PIE

MAKES ONE
9-INCH PIE

Some pies lend themselves more readily to a vegan treatment than others. Fruit pies, with fillings thickened by starch or pectin rather than eggs or gelatin, don't require many tweaks in order to be completely plant based. But a custard pie, which by definition contains eggs and dairy, certainly doesn't sound like it could be vegan-friendly. And yet, this is a truly excellent riff on Mom's Lemon Custard Pie (page 176), with no egg cracking or milk pouring required.

1. To make the crust: In a large bowl, combine the flour, cane sugar, and salt. Using a pastry blender, cut in the vegan butter until crumbly. Add 1 tablespoon of the ice water and use a spoon to stir it into the mixture, working the dough just enough so that it comes together, and adding a little more water if needed. Dump the dough onto the counter and press it out into a disk. Wrap it in plastic wrap and refrigerate.

2. Preheat the oven to 375°F.

3. Roll out the crust, and lay it in a 9-inch pie pan. Use the tines of a fork to poke holes in the bottom and sides, which will keep the crust from bubbling. Trim and flute the edge according to the instructions on page 23. (A crust made with vegan butter will handle like Moe's.) Bake for 35 to 40 minutes, or until golden brown. Set aside to cool completely.

4. To make the filling: In a medium saucepan, combine the lemon juice, cane sugar, and agar agar. Bring to a boil over medium heat, stirring constantly, and cook for 5 minutes, or until the mixture is thick and no longer grainy. Remove from the heat and set aside.

5. In the top of a double boiler, or a heatproof bowl nestled into a saucepan with simmering water below, combine the white chocolate chips and vegan butter, stirring until completely melted. Remove from the heat.

6. Whisking constantly, slowly pour the lemon mixture into the melted white chocolate, and continue whisking until well combined. Add the yogurt and whisk to incorporate.

7. Pour the filling into the piecrust. Refrigerate for at least 2 hours before serving, so the pie can set completely. Serve cold. Garnish with confectioners' sugar if desired.

Crust

2 cups all-purpose flour

⅓ cup organic cane sugar

½ teaspoon kosher salt

½ cup vegan butter (I like Country Crock plant butter)

1 to 2 tablespoons ice water

Filling

¼ cup freshly squeezed lemon juice

¾ cup organic cane sugar

2½ teaspoons agar agar powder

1 cup vegan white chocolate chips

3 tablespoons vegan butter or shortening

3 tablespoons dairy-free yogurt

Confectioners' sugar for garnish (optional)

CHAPTER 6

nut pies

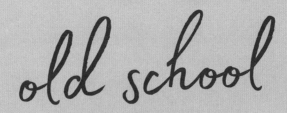

old school

There might not be as many nut pies as there are fruit pies, but they are mighty as a group, arguably the pinnacle of holiday pie baking. We always make Pecan Pie (page 202) during the holidays, and my memories of baking at Thanksgiving and Christmas will forever be connected with that wonderfully gooey, crunchy pie. It's up there with pumpkin and sweet potato for being *the* holiday pie.

But nut pies don't begin and end with pecans. Pies made with peanuts and peanut butter bring to mind after-school snacks in the best of ways. And then there are the refined nuts, such as hazelnuts, which taste wonderful with chocolate in Chocolate-Hazelnut Pie (page 205), and walnuts, my mom's favorite, which pops up in the very new school crust of the Salted Chocolate Pie with Walnut Crust and Pomegranates (page 213).

PECAN PIE

½ cup salted margarine
or butter (if you must)

1 tablespoon all-purpose
flour

2 eggs

1 teaspoon vanilla extract

1½ cups dark corn syrup

1 cup pecans

½ recipe Moe's Piecrust
(page 19)

In the late 1980s and early '90s, I worked the third shift at a cardboard box factory in New Jersey. Those were long nights, running a machine that made cardboard inserts for packaging bottles and packing up hundreds and hundreds of boxes. But there were good people who worked at the factory, and we'd get a bit of time to relax and chat in the break room while we got yet another cup of coffee. It was far from a comfortable place, with its hard, straight-backed chairs and harsh fluorescent lights. But a break was a break. When my shift was wrapping up in the morning, the office staff began showing up, and we'd sometimes overlap. That's how I first met the young Black woman who worked as a secretary, and she and I bonded over pie. (Nearly thirty years later, her name, unfortunately, escapes me.) Usually the factory floor and office workers didn't interact all that much, but she'd come into our break room and we'd talk about baking. She was from the South—Georgia, I believe—and shared this family recipe for pecan pie. I've used it ever since. You could swap out the margarine for butter, but I can't bring myself to make the change. This pie always makes me think of her, and our chats about pie, all those years ago.

1. Preheat the oven to 375°F.

2. In a medium saucepan, melt the margarine over low heat. Add the flour and stir until smooth. Remove from the heat and let cool for 15 minutes. Stir in the eggs and vanilla and continue stirring until completely incorporated. Stir in the corn syrup and pecans.

3. Roll out the crust, and lay it in a 9-inch pie pan. Trim and flute the edge according to the instructions on page 23. Pour the pecan mixture into the pie shell.

4. Bake for 45 minutes, or until the top is browned and the center no longer jiggles. Cool on the counter until room temperature, 2 to 3 hours, and serve.

PEANUT BUTTER PIE

Graham Cracker Piecrust
(page 29)

6 ounces cream cheese,
at room temperature

2½ cups confectioners'
sugar

½ cup creamy peanut
butter

2 tablespoons whole milk

1 cup heavy cream

2 tablespoons peanuts,
finely chopped

No recipe box in a Pennsylvania kitchen is complete without an index card devoted to this pie. There are many different versions. Some have a baked filling made with butter or sweetened condensed milk, while others have a filling cooked on the stove top. I tried many of them before landing on this recipe, which is very simple and straightforward: You smoosh together cream cheese and peanut butter, sweeten it, and then fold in whipped cream to make a nice, airy filling. It's the kind of pie you can easily make for a weeknight dinner. We have a bunch of peanut butter lovers in the family, so this pie is often requested for family get-togethers and birthday parties, which I certainly don't mind— because I love to eat it, too.

1. Prepare and bake the graham cracker crust. Set aside.

2. In a large bowl, use an electric mixer on medium speed to beat the cream cheese until it is soft and creamy. Turn down the mixer speed to low, and add the confectioners' sugar, beating to blend it into the cream cheese. Return the mixer speed to medium and beat the cream cheese mixture until uniform and smooth, about 3 minutes more. Add the peanut butter and milk, and continue beating until well combined. Set aside.

3. In a medium bowl, with clean beaters, use the electric mixer to beat the cream until soft peaks form. Fold the whipped cream into the peanut butter mixture, one-third at a time.

4. Scoop the filling into the graham cracker crust and refrigerate for at least 3 hours. Garnish with the chopped peanuts before serving.

CHOCOLATE-HAZELNUT PIE

MAKES ONE
9-INCH PIE

This pie is an oddball—it doesn't have a crust. Rest assured, that doesn't make it a cake. As the pie bakes, the edges get a little crispy, so you notice a distinct textural difference between the outside and the middle, just as you would with a pastry crust. And do semantics really matter when we're talking about the classic combination of chocolate and hazelnuts?

1. Preheat the oven to 350°F.

2. To make the filling: Put the hazelnuts on a baking sheet in a single layer and roast for 15 minutes, shaking the pan a few times halfway through roasting. The skins will start to peel away from the nuts, and the flesh underneath should look golden brown. Remove from the oven and dump the hazelnuts onto a clean kitchen towel (careful, they'll be very hot!). Wrap them up and let sit for a few minutes. Then rub the nuts with the towel to remove the skins. Set aside for about 30 minutes to cool.

3. In a food processor, combine half of the chocolate, the cooled hazelnuts, and the flour. Pulse until the nuts are coarsely chopped. Transfer to a medium bowl and set aside.

4. Add the remaining half of the chocolate and the granulated sugar to the food processor and process until fine. Add the hot water, eggs, ½ cup plus 1 tablespoon of the butter, the vanilla, and cinnamon. Process until blended. Add the reserved hazelnut mixture to the food processor and pulse once or twice to mix.

5. Use the remaining 1 tablespoon butter to generously grease a 9-inch pie pan and dust with flour. Pour in the filling and bake for 35 to 40 minutes, or until the top looks firm and lightly browned. Cool on the counter for at least 1 hour.

6. To make the spiced whipped cream: Before serving, in a medium bowl, use an electric mixer to beat the cream with the confectioners' sugar, vanilla, and cinnamon until soft peaks form.

7. Serve the pie at room temperature, garnishing each slice with a dollop of the whipped cream.

Filling

1 cup raw hazelnuts

8 ounces semisweet chocolate, coarsely chopped

¼ cup all-purpose flour, plus more for dusting the pie pan

¾ cup granulated sugar

¼ cup very hot water

4 eggs

½ cup plus 2 tablespoons salted butter

2 teaspoons vanilla extract

½ teaspoon ground cinnamon

Spiced Whipped Cream

1 cup heavy cream

2 tablespoons confectioners' sugar

2 teaspoons vanilla extract

¼ teaspoon ground cinnamon

new school

One of the most noticeable shifts in contemporary baking is the embrace of salt in the pastry kitchen. Instead of suggesting the standard tiny, barely discernible amount (which, by the way, helps baked goods brown better and remain fresh longer), many recipes now have a savory edge, thanks to an extra pinch or two. As a flavor enhancer, salt makes everything around it taste better, even sweet flavors. A detectable amount of salt in a dessert helps to balance flavors, as well. And in a pie with nuts, it's kind of a no-brainer: Nuts taste great with salt; they taste great with sugar; and they taste amazing with both. In this section, we celebrate pies with salted caramel, salted peanuts, and a garnish of crunchy flakes of sea salt.

SALTED CARAMEL PECAN

6 tablespoons salted butter

1 cup corn syrup

2 cups packed dark brown sugar

2 eggs

2 teaspoons vanilla extract

¾ teaspoon kosher salt

½ recipe Moe's Piecrust (page 19)

1 cup pecans

There's really no improving on a great Pecan Pie (page 202), so think of this version as an homage instead. The filling is a little bit richer, thanks to the addition of the eggs, and the caramel flavor is a little more intense. Add a healthy pinch of salt to the filling, and you've got a contemporary version of the classic.

1. Preheat the oven to 350°F.

2. In a medium saucepan, melt the butter over medium heat. Pour in the corn syrup and whisk to combine. Transfer to a large bowl. Whisk in the brown sugar, stirring until no lumps remain. Add the eggs, vanilla, and salt, and whisk until well blended. Set the caramel aside.

3. Roll out the crust, and lay it in a 9-inch pie pan. Trim and flute the edge according to the instructions on page 23. Place the pecans in a single layer across the bottom of the crust. Pour the caramel over the pecans.

4. Bake for 40 minutes, or until the filling has risen to the top edge of the crust and the top is beginning to crack. Cool on the counter until room temperature, about 2 hours, and serve.

CHOCOLATE–PEANUT BUTTER BANOFFEE PIE

I love the trick of baking sweetened condensed milk to make the toffee for this pie (for the unfamiliar, banana + toffee = banoffee). The process makes sense: Expose the sugary milk to heat for a long enough period of time, and eventually it will caramelize and become nice and thick. Still, every time I take a panful out of the oven, it feels like magic. The sweetened condensed milk is transformed into a rich, sticky toffee that, of course, tastes delicious alongside chocolate, peanut butter, and bananas!

1. Preheat the oven to 300°F.

2. Pour the sweetened condensed milk into a 9-inch square glass baking dish. Cover tightly with aluminum foil, and place in a larger roasting pan filled with enough water to come halfway up the side of the baking dish. Bake for 3 hours, or until the sweetened condensed milk is thickened and caramelized. This is your toffee. Remove from the oven and cool completely, about 1 hour. Increase the oven temperature to 350°F.

3. In a food processor, pulse the cookies, cream filling and all, until finely ground. Transfer to a large bowl, add the chopped peanuts and butter, and stir to combine. Dump the "dough" into a 9-inch pie pan, and use your fingertips to press it evenly over the bottom and up the sides of the pan. You want to make sure the thickness of the crust is uniform, particularly where the bottom meets the side. Bake for 15 minutes, and immediately press out the crust again with the back of a metal spoon if the sides slip down. Set aside to cool completely.

4. In a large bowl, combine 2¼ cups of the cream and the sugar. Use an electric mixer on medium-high speed to beat the cream until it holds stiff peaks. Put the peanut butter in another large bowl. Fold in the whipped cream, one-quarter at a time, until completely incorporated. Refrigerate until the pie is ready for assembly.

continued ⟶

Two 14-ounce cans sweetened condensed milk

17 cream-filled chocolate sandwich cookies (such as Oreos)

1 cup salted dry-roasted peanuts, chopped

6 tablespoons salted butter, melted

2¼ cups plus 2 tablespoons heavy cream

⅓ cup sugar

⅔ cup creamy peanut butter

8 ounces semisweet chocolate, chopped

4 ripe bananas

1 tablespoon unsweetened cocoa powder

5. Put the chopped chocolate in a small heatproof bowl. In a small saucepan, heat the remaining 2 tablespoons cream over medium heat until bubbles form around the edge and the cream begins to steam. Pour the scalded cream over the chocolate and stir until completely melted.

6. Spoon the cooled toffee into the piecrust and spread it out into an even layer. Slice the bananas and arrange them over the toffee. Pour the chocolate ganache over the bananas, and top with the peanut butter whipped cream for the final layer. Refrigerate for at least 4 hours. Before serving, sift the cocoa powder over the top of the pie.

SALTED CHOCOLATE PIE WITH WALNUT CRUST AND POMEGRANATES

MAKES ONE 9-INCH PIE

Between the walnuts, the salt, and the olive oil drizzled on the top, this pie has a number of savory touches that I just love. The olive oil is scant, but it gives the top a nice shine, and helps the salt and the pomegranates to adhere to it. And the bright, almost grassy flavor plays really well with the rich chocolate filling and the tart crunch of the pomegranates. When I eat this pie, I can never stop myself at one slice.

1. Preheat the oven to 350°F.

2. To make the crust: In a food processor, pulse the walnuts until finely ground. Add the butter, sugar, and salt, and blend until the mixture comes together into a soft dough. Dump the dough onto a sheet of plastic wrap, form it into a ball, bundle it up, and refrigerate for at least 1 hour.

3. Put the dough in a 9-inch pie pan, and press it into the bottom and up the sides of the dish. Use the tines of a fork to poke several holes in the dough. Refrigerate for 30 minutes. Bake for 20 to 25 minutes, or until the bottom looks shiny with the melted butter. Set aside to cool.

4. To make the filling: In a saucepan, heat the milk, butter, and chocolate over low heat until the butter and chocolate both melt. Set aside. In a medium heatproof bowl, beat together the egg yolks, sugar, cornstarch, and salt. Whisk in a few splashes of the warm milk to temper the eggs, and then pour the mixture into the pan. Bring to a boil over medium heat, stirring constantly, and continue to boil, stirring, for 3 minutes longer. Remove from the heat and add the vanilla.

5. Pour the chocolate filling into the walnut crust and cool on a wire rack for 2 hours, then refrigerate for 2 hours. Just before serving, drizzle the pie with the olive oil and scatter the pomegranates and sea salt over the filling.

Crust

2½ cups raw walnuts

4 tablespoon salted butter, at room temperature

3 tablespoons sugar

½ teaspoon kosher salt

Filling

4 cups whole milk

2 tablespoons salted butter

3 ounces unsweetened chocolate, chopped

4 egg yolks

1 cup sugar

¼ cup cornstarch

Hefty pinch of kosher salt

2 teaspoons vanilla extract

1 teaspoon olive oil

¼ cup pomegranate arils

Maldon sea salt (or another large-crystal finishing salt)

AFTERWORD

When the first Pie Hole opened in 2011, the Arts District in downtown Los Angeles wasn't the sort of place where you saw a lot of strollers. For years it had been a neighborhood of old loft studios, where painters, sculptors, and other artists worked. Then a few coffee spots and bars appeared, and eventually, restaurants. There were plenty of fancy apartments, too, by the time we arrived in the neighborhood, but they were more like the Arts District loft in the TV show *New Girl*—full of young people who were sharing. But it didn't matter if we weren't in a family neighborhood; we were going to be a family shop, just like the little pie shop on the corner that I had dreamed of all those years ago.

I may have been new to the business of a bakery, but for me pie and family have always been basically one and the same. Moe taught me to bake pie, and I taught my kids. And, of course, we ate those pies together, too. The shop would carry on that tradition by sharing our family recipes with anyone and everyone who came through the door. And it continued more directly through my grandson, Jordan, and the baking we would do together in the Pie Hole kitchen whenever he came to town for a visit.

Jordan was always coming up with wacky ideas for pies. He would say things like, "Oh, Mimi, we could make a pie out of tree bark!"—inspired by whatever was in his line of sight. We worked on pies together that were a bit more feasible, like the S'mores Pie (page 139) he dreamed up. Other times, we were coming up with pies that reflected Jordan's quirky taste, like the Mac 'n' Cheese Pie (opposite). The way I saw it, the more pies we had on the menu that were a product of the times we spent together in the kitchen, the more the Pie Hole would feel like a family place, rather than just a bakery where you could buy a kid a slice of pie. I like to think that it worked.

AFTERWORD PIE:
MAC 'N' CHEESE PIE

MAKES ONE
9-INCH PIE

We came up with this version of the recipe with the help of former Pie Hole chef Jeffrey Froehlich when Jordan was going through that period that all kids go through, when all they eat is pasta. So why not make a pasta pie for all of the Jordans out there? It has been on the menu since day one, and has been an even bigger hit with adults than with kids. Now that he's twenty, Jordan is a more adventurous eater. But he still loves this pie.

¾ cup elbow macaroni

1 tablespoon salted butter

¼ cup diced onions

Scant ½ cup whole milk

3 tablespoons heavy cream

½ teaspoon Dijon mustard

1 teaspoon kosher salt

Freshly ground
black pepper

1 cup grated sharp
Cheddar cheese

½ cup grated Velveeta
cheese

½ recipe Moe's Piecrust
(page 19)

Panko bread crumbs

1. Bring a medium pot of salted water to a boil. Add the macaroni and cook until al dente, about 6 minutes. The macaroni should still be slightly firm. Drain and run cold water over the macaroni until cooled. Spread out on a cookie sheet (so they don't stick together), and refrigerate while you make the cheese sauce.

2. In a medium saucepan, melt the butter over low heat and add the onions. Cook until the onions are caramelized and dark in color, 15 to 20 minutes. Add the milk, cream, mustard, salt, and a few grinds of pepper. Bring the milk to a simmer and add the Cheddar and Velveeta. Cook, whisking, until the cheeses are completely melted. Remove from the heat, and add the macaroni to the cheese sauce, stirring well with a spatula. Set aside.

3. Preheat the oven to 375°F.

4. Roll out the crust, and lay it in a 9-inch pie pan. Trim and flute the edge according to the instructions on page 23. Fill the crust with the mac 'n' cheese, and sprinkle with panko bread crumbs.

5. Bake for 35 to 40 minutes, or until the bread crumbs are browned. Serve hot.

ABOUT THE CONTRIBUTORS

With more than fifty years of pie-baking experience, **Becky Grasley** is many things to the Pie Hole: co-owner/founder, matriarch, recipe-keeper, pie mom. After a career in nursing, Becky opened the first the Pie Hole L.A. in the Arts District location with her retirement savings. She's still baking today, creating new recipes in the kitchen of the very house where she grew up, in Nescopeck, Pennsylvania, and tasting every new flavor that we create. She's the one who taught us that pie is love, and she makes sure our guests are happy with every bite. She is the mother of two grown children and grandmother to Jordan, her only grandson, who is her smile.

Sean Brennan is a seasoned restaurant veteran of thirty years and the co-founder and CEO of the Pie Hole, which celebrated its ten-year anniversary in 2021. Sean developed the first-of-its-kind bakery entrepreneur accelerator program called the Pie Lab, designed to help underserved and marginalized bakery entrepreneurs. He has also designed and implemented innovative hospitality culture programs such as Service Leadership and Care for Crew leadership initiatives. When Sean is not practicing his Japanese at the Pie Hole locations in Tokyo, he is spending time with his family, geeking out about wine, obsessing about hospitality, and making the best damn pie in the world.

For more than a decade, **Willy Blackmore** has covered the food world as a journalist. He has been honored by the Association of Food Journalists and nominated for awards by the International Association of Culinary Professionals and the Los Angeles Press Club. His writing has been published by *New York,* the *Los Angeles Times,* the *New York Times Magazine, Eater, Down East* magazine, and elsewhere. Born and raised in Iowa, he grew up in Pie Country and now lives in Brooklyn, New York.

ACKNOWLEDGMENTS

To everyone who has touched my life and helped shape me into who I have become, and to those who came into my life to make this cookbook a reality—thank you, all!

To my angels in heaven, my loving and kind brother, Bob Pursel (1949–2011), whose encouragement and love throughout my life gave me confidence to keep trying. Knowing you always had my back made us closer as we navigated life. My father, Atwood Pursel (1928–2013), for his support and kindness and sense of humor. My most special grandmother, Helen (Mom) Pursel (1907–1993), for her unconditional and complete love, making every minute I spent with her all about me and giving me the courage to try new things. My businesslike grandmother, Grace (Moe) Kacyon (1897–1975), for teaching me, in her way, all about listening and respect and, most important to love baking pies.

Sean K. Brennan, thank you for being the man you are and my partner. One who makes promises and keeps them and walks the walk of honesty and commitment. You are patient and you always take the time to listen, which calms me, centers me, and helps me to expand on ideas and suggestions without fear of rebuke. There should be a picture of you next to "due diligence" in the dictionary because you, always, always do your homework! You are a wonderful father to Pia and husband to Allison, and you flawlessly keep your priorities straight. My dream of my pie shop would have sputtered and died without you, and I will be forever grateful that you are in my life.

Willy Blackmore, I do not know where to begin. Ours certainly was a match made in heaven. You are patient, so kind, and considerate. The way you adapted to my unusual way of communicating was nothing short of wonderful. You not only listened intently and helped to pen my actual thoughts and stories into words, you got me. You worked around the many power outages, internet interruptions, my need to use texting instead of emails, and scheduling delays. You are diligent and smart, and could roll with whatever the challenges of my life happened to be at the time. You are an amazing man and wonderful human being. I now consider you a cherished friend.

Edie Ames, for hitting the fast-forward button on this project. The cookbook suddenly got wings when you were at the helm steering us. Your broad visions took into account all things while we were in our tunnel-vision mode, trying to mold a business we were proud of while missing the finer points of creation. This cookbook suddenly became included in the list of priorities. Plus, you found a way to make pie holes an actual menu item!

Bianca Molina, you're a thoughtful, hardworking, much loved human being. My world is a better place with you in it. You started out as one of our baristas and made your way up in the company to our current director of operations. Your heart shows up wherever you look in the shops and spaces of the Pie Hole L.A. You are instrumental in keeping our brand and our story in the front of everyone's minds. You truly love being a part of this journey, and it shows up in everything you touch. I trust you completely with keeping it all real as each location opens. You were there in Japan and also Saudi Arabia to train and teach our business culture and techniques. You have an artsy, creative side and add beauty to the pies with touches of genius (like putting the candied lemon slices on top of the Lemon Chess Pie instead of inside).

Thank you to the amazing Ten Speed team: Dervla, who grew up a good bit of her youth in northeastern Pennsylvania, making her so relatable to my own upbringing. Understanding the nuances of my background gave her a most patient and knowledgeable perspective on where I was coming from. My life's story and these recipes came from my heart, and you made my vision a reality. "Thank you" seems like not enough. I should bake you pies!

Emma, you took the time to come to the photo shoot. I will never forget that. I was beyond nervous and you addressed my anxiety by just being there, telling me it was going just the way it should be and that we were getting it right. This was my first-ever photo shoot, and you made me extremely calm and secure as it continued to unfold.

Ashley considered my limited technical abilities and physically mailed the pages as they became my book, for my review! Who does that anymore? Actually seeing and handling the pages as they became available was so helpful, and you will never truly understand what it meant to me to share this process with my mother. My hope was that this cookbook would be published in her lifetime and, as the years ticked by during the process, I worried that would not happen. It meant so much for my mother to see the pages as they were mailed back and forth.

Sarah Smith of the David Black Agency in New York, I keep coming back to patience. You made every question I asked seem like an important one. I am old and so not techy, and you adjusted to me. I know that Sean found you, but you made me feel like I knew you forever. The proposal pitch was so spot on and true to my vision that it made me cry to read it. I feel like we made memories usually shared only with close family.

CHEFS

Adrianna Sullivan—the very first chef! Your talent blew me away, and you made an impact on me for sure. I had never worked with a chef before, and I am glad you were my first experience.

Jeffrey Froehlich—My love for you is forever! You are an amazingly calm, sincere person, and your experience and commitment coupled with your desire to get it right will never be forgotten. Your smile is always cherished, and you share it often. I am so glad you came into my life.

Sarah Chaffin—Your creativity and kindness coupled with your sincerity made you easy to know and work with. You brought not only delicious pies but also polish and beauty to the menu.

Beth Kellerhals—The phrase "a little bit country and a little bit rock and roll" always reminds me of you. You took country (me) and rock and roll (you) and combined them into wonderfulness. You always began with a family recipe and tweaked it into a pie with unusual fare!

Ana Bayon—Kind, sweet, and talented! Plus, you came back to me after some time apart! I love being in the kitchen with you and hope that we have many, many years doing just that.

Lizbeth Solis—You picked up some pretty broken pieces and put them back together in the current production kitchen, and it will not ever be forgotten.

Anthony Tahlier, you were serious when it counted and spot on with knowing when I needed to take a minute and get a hug. Your unique way of controlling the many personalities without being too obvious made our many days of shooting so enjoyable. Your talent made photos of my family pies into works of art.

Emily Johnson is another employee who became a valuable and trusted asset. Her beautiful mind is so structured and attentive and her culinary background saved us during a difficult transition period. "Can't" is not in her vocabulary, as she rolls up her sleeves and takes every task thrown at her to completion of a job done well. She is charming and respectful, allowing her Southern upbringing to shine. I am so grateful she now is a part of our management team.

To my Ben, for loving me just the way I am. "Kind" and "strong" are just two adjectives that sing out to me when I think of Ben. He keeps me calm, and he loves pie! I am so grateful he is persistent and consistent in his love.

To my mother, who I call Me-Mudder, for living and giving and loving in her advanced years. She likes to tell people her age by beginning with "I am only [such and such] years old" because she still feels and acts young. She is an inspiration of energy and works daily to keep her home and gardens perfect. I hope I am as good as she is when I grow up.

Finally, last but not least, to my grandson, Jordan. I do it all for you, my love.

INDEX

All rights reserved.
Published in the United States by Ten Speed Press,
an imprint of Random House, a division of Penguin Random House LLC, New York.
TenSpeed.com
RandomHouseBooks.com

Ten Speed Press and the Ten Speed Press colophon are registered
trademarks of Penguin Random House LLC.

Typefaces: Font Fabric's Madelyn, Laura Worthington's Fairwater Sans,
Monotype's Playland, and ParaType's PT Sans Pro

Library of Congress Cataloging-in-Publication Data is on file with the publisher.

Hardcover ISBN: 978-1-9848-6050-7
eBook ISBN: 978-1-9848-6051-4

Printed in China

Acquiring editor: Dervla Kelly | Production editor: Ashley Pierce
Designer: Ashley Lima | Art director: Emma Campion
Production designers: Mari Gill and Faith Hague
Production and prepress color manager: Jane Chinn
Food stylist: Caroline Hwang | Food stylist assistant: Jessica Darakjian
Prop stylist: Nidia Cueva | Photo assistant: Phoebe Solomon
Copyeditor: Deborah Kops | Proofreaders: Deborah Geline and
Linda Bouchard | Indexer: Ken DellaPenta
Marketer: Stephanie Davis

10 9 8 7 6 5 4 3 2 1

First Edition